THE YACHTSMAN'S GUIDE TO
better maintenance
by Bill Duggan

YACHTING/BOATING BOOKS • ZIFF-DAVIS PUBLISHING
COMPANY   NEW YORK

*To Peg, who shared my love of boats
and our happy hours aboard them.*

W. E. D.

Acknowledgements

The author and publisher would like to thank the following manufacturers who contributed photos, drawings and other material:

Cummins Engine Company, Inc.
Detroit Diesel Allison
   Division of General Motors Corporation
Edson Corp.
International Paint Company, Inc.
Koehler Co.
Lewmar Marine, Inc.
Merriman Holbrook, Inc.
Narco/Barient
Volvo Penta of America

Acknowledgement is also made to Charles Scribner's Sons for permission to reprint copyrighted material from their publication of *The Wind In The Willows* by Kenneth Grahame.

Contents

Keeping Up the Boat

Like everyone who owns a boat, you probably soon learned to play this game with the object of enjoying as much time afloat without spending an undue amount of labor and money doing the maintenance. If you have a fat checkbook, a boatyard or marina can be relied on to do the work. But if you're in the same club as most skippers who can't afford this luxury, the answer is to do as much of the upkeep yourself to keep the cost down.

Whether you or a yard does the maintenance, it is important to do it right for several reasons. Safety is the most important of these, for in an emergency your own safety and that of everyone aboard may depend on a critical piece of equipment and how well it has been kept up. From another viewpoint, good maintenance protects your investment in the boat and, with inflation today, the replacement cost may equal or exceed that of your home. Still on the financial side, it is often cheaper (and far more efficient) to do preventive maintenance and avoid expensive repairs or replacement when equipment breaks down completely.

Whether your pride and joy is power or sail, the purpose of this guide is to point out what to refit, repair or replace during the annual maintenance at a haulout or fitting-out after a layup and storage. Most of the work should be within your expertise if you're reasonably handy with tools or have the desire to learn.

In doing the upkeep, there are a few ground rules to follow that will pay off in time saved and less blood, sweat and tears all around. The first is to keep a maintenance log and list all repairs as they are needed or as you notice them. With this list you can set up a work schedule, assign priorities and plan jobs well in advance by dividing them into "I'll-Do-It-Myself" and "Have-a-Pro-Handle" columns. In deciding, make sure you have the skills to do the work. Saving money by doing it yourself is a good idea but it's often wiser and in the long run cheaper to let a pro handle the job. They usually do a better job and in less time. You'll also be able to spend more time enjoying the boat and less fixing it.

In using the guide, you'll find the maintenance it covers has been divided into the boat's logical work areas listed in the table of contents. The objective is to give you a handy, practical source of how-to information about everything from masthead to keel, to have aboard for on-the-spot use in keeping your boat shipshape and in Bristol fashion.

1. The Hull Work

"There is *nothing*—absolutely nothing—half as much worth doing as simply messing about in boats . . . or *with* boats . . . In or out of 'em, it doesn't matter."

What the Water Rat said about his boat in Kenneth Grahame's *The Wind In The Willows,* is also true of yours. The job of keeping up your boat may involve more than "simply messing about" but it's worth doing for the enjoyment when she's in the water. It may seem like tackling a mountain when you start the maintenance but it really isn't if you go after the molehills—those smaller jobs it can be broken down into, most of which you can handle yourself.

Since work on the hull is the most important part of any maintenance program you decide on, begin with this first. The other areas can slide for a season or even two, but unless the hull is in good condition, the rest of your work may go for naught.

The Washdown

Whether hull care is done at the annual haulout or before storage, the first thing to be done should be a thorough washdown from truck to keel. Use a mild detergent or a biodegradable cleaner like Sudbury's Boat Soap, with a stiff brush and warm water. On the stubborn spots, one of the specialty cleaners like Star Brite (in both marine polish and "Vinyl-Brite") will help. The washdown may slow you up a bit but get it all done at one time instead of having to go back again because dirt from the deck cleaning has run down the hull sides.

Bottom Cleaning and Sanding

Since neither time, tide nor teredos wait for any man, begin bottom care within an hour or two after hauling, while the growth is still soft. Have the yard steam clean it or use a stiff brush, dull scraper and a hose to flush off the crud. Use bronze wool or a pad of old screening on the tough spots. Above all, avoid digging into the old bottom paint and the gel coat on fiberglass.

When the bottom is dry, sand everything below the boot top with a medium-grit paper and a power sander. Watch the edges so you don't gouge through the old paint into the surface beneath it. Wear a hat, mask and goggles when you do the sanding because some antifouling paints are toxic and the dust may cause blindness. After the sanding is done, hose off the bottom and let it dry. Now is a good time to give the surface a real in-depth inspection for damages which should be marked for repairs with a china pencil. We'll cover these later in this section.

Fiberglass Hull Care

When this material was first introduced, some sales-minded people gave buyers the idea that fiberglass hulls would be maintenance-free, thus doing a disservice to the industry. Fiberglass *does* require upkeep but a lot less than

Figure 1. Steam cleaning at annual haulout removes marine growth before it can harden. A stiff brush, detergent and hose will also do the job.

wood or metal hulls. A brief outline of fiberglass construction may help to explain this and also how it can be damaged and repaired.

The hull is built in a mould starting with the outside layer or gel coat, a shiny surface with the color. Successive layers of glass fabric saturated with resin are then laid up to form a thick laminate that produces a strong hull, impervious to rot. Where more strength and rigidity are needed, a core of cellular plastic or wood is moulded into the hull. It is important to remember that cracks and damage to the gel coat can let water attack the layers beneath and strip them apart—a process known as "delamination." This may spread and weaken the hull—sounds a bit gloomy but if caught in time it can be repaired without any permanent damage to the boat.

CLEANING THE TOPSIDES

After the overall washdown, clean off any oil, algae, creosote, etc., with something like "Boatlife" or "MDR" and a slightly abrasive pad, such as "Scotch-Brite," used with care. Check the gel coat and again mark damaged spots for later repair. If there's no surface damage, finish the care treatment by waxing and polishing. Slight blemishes can be buffed out with a rubbing compound.

Where the gel coat has weathered, the original lustre can sometimes be restored with a light sanding to remove chalking and oxidation. But do it carefully so you don't go through the color, and finish off the job with waxing and polishing. If it looks like the weathering is too far gone or too extensive, you may have to consider painting the fiberglass. This often happens after several years of exposure.

REPAIRING FIBERGLASS DAMAGE

While this material is tough and strong, fiberglass hulls are still vulnerable to some forms of damage. This can run the gamut from simple surface cracks and holes, which the average owner can fix, to more critical damage such as delamination and punctures of the hull. We'll touch on both types and suggest remedial action for do-it-yourself jobs and those best left to an expert.

SURFACE REPAIRS

These usually involve scuffs, gouges, small cracks, holes, etc. Slight ones like abrasion marks and hairline cracks can sometimes be buffed out with rubbing compound. Where the cracks are deeper, clean and widen them out to a "V" shape, then fill with a ready-made epoxy or polyester putty. You can make your own material with resin and chopped fibers or a thickening agent. For gel coat repairs, use one of the kits for this purpose. Polyester is easier to work with, but epoxy has more strength and bonds better. With either, fill the damaged

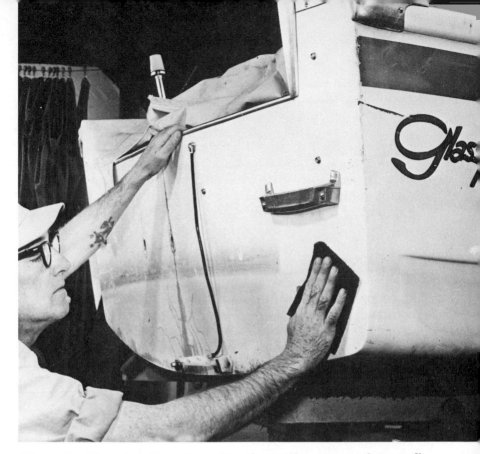

Figure 2. Cleaning fiberglass. Synthetic abrasive pad gets off topsides dirt and waterline crust. Pads will also help restore color and gloss to gel coat by using them, carefully, with rubbing compound.

areas slightly higher than the surface to allow for shrinking, then sand it flush and prime.

OTHER DAMAGES

The most serious of these in a fiberglass hull usually comes from an impact that breaks the gel coat. Moving water can then strip away the layers underneath, causing delamination. Since the repair involves rebuilding the layers, unless you have the expertise, the job should be done by a specialist. This kind of damage can quickly spread so have it fixed before the boat goes back in the water.

An impact, if hard enough, can also crack the laminate or even puncture it, thus weakening the hull structure. Here again, patching the area calls for a high degree of skill, so if you don't have it, call in a pro.

PAINTING FIBERGLASS

Because the surface of polyester resin is so smooth and hard, preparing it for painting is different than that of wood —in fact, closer to painting metal. The surface of fiberglass often has to be slightly etched either by sanding or with a chemical primer which softens up the gel coat enough to get good adhesion. If the glass hasn't been painted before, a solvent may be necessary to remove any mould-release agent and wax still remaining on the hull before painting is begun.

THE TOPSIDES

While the gel coat will usually keep its color and lustre for a number of seasons provided it is cleaned, waxed and polished, in time it will become discolored from water stains and begin to look tacky. That's when it's time to think of painting and restoring the old girl's good looks. The two-part epoxy and polyurethane paints have some advantages when used on fiberglass because they provide a strong, flexible coating with good abrasion resistance. The rub with them is they're tricky to apply and require a dust-free atmosphere during the painting. If you want a finish to equal the original glass in color, sheen and hardness, have a professional do the job—it's well worth the money.

THE BOTTOM AND BOOT TOP

Here's the place where you can paint fiberglass yourself

with very little fuss and feathers. Before you start on the bottom though, decide how you want to do the boot top. Some owners prefer using a colored plastic tape for this, while others choose to paint the top. If you go the tape route, you can apply it after the bottom paint is dry. To paint the boot top, mask off above and below it with tape then lay on the finish you've selected. Remember to take off the tape before it dries hard or you'll mess up the edges of the boot top.

On painting the bottom, we'll assume you've cleaned and sanded it. As a preliminary step, select an antifouling paint that's compatible with the old finish. The Paint Chart at the end of this section will help on this. Mask off the boot top with tape and then lay on a smooth, even coat of bottom paint, working it close to the underwater hardware like shaft struts, rudder fittings, etc. If you haven't used a roller on the bottom before, let yourself in for a treat and save time and labor. A fuzzy kind that holds a lot of paint is best. You'll get a fine spray from the roller so wear gloves, a hat and goggles as well as a mask because some of the paints are toxic and can affect your skin, eyes and lungs.

Wooden Hull Care

While the trend is toward wider use of glass and some metal in hull materials, there are still many owners who prefer wood, even though it is harder to maintain. The fact that with proper care a wooden hull will last a long time, is amply proven by the number of boats still giving yeoman's service after many years afloat.

If you're a wooden boat afficionado and want to keep your pride and joy in good condition, here are the places where maintenance is important along with how-to suggestions for the work:

CLEANING TOPSIDES AND BOTTOM

Your overall washdown is a good starting place for cleaning topsides, but you should concentrate on any fender marks, grease, dockside rubbings, etc., using bronze wool and a detergent. While you're cleaning look for gouges, cracks, splits, sprung planks and loose fastenings, spotting them with a china marker. Damp spots and flaking paint may be symptoms of dry rot beneath—we'll get into this later. After cleaning and sanding, the bottom should be ready for any repair work you may have spotted.

PATCHING AND REPAIRS

To fill in surface damages, use a trowelling compound or one of the polyester-resin putties—though harder to work with, they do a better job. Remove loose bungs or cracked filling over fastenings, check for corrosion, and tighten the screw or bolt. Badly corroded metal should be replaced if possible. If not, fill up the hole over the fastening, and put in a new one as close to the old as possible, covering it with a bung or compound. A sprung or split strake in the planking is tricky to replace, so let a pro do it.

SEAMS AND CAULKING

Where those in the hull need attention, remove the old caulking and clean out the seam. A good tool for this job is an old file, heated and bent into a hook, then ground to a point that will just fit in the seam. If the old cotton is good, leave it alone—if not, tap in new cotton at the bottom of the seam. An old putty knife with a ground-down blade makes a good tool. Fill in the seam with one of the silicon-rubber or poly-sulphide sealants, using a caulking gun or putty knife. Masking tape on either side of the seam makes it easier to fill with a gun but wastes expensive sealant. The putty-knife method is slower and takes longer to do—take your pick.

DRY ROT

A book could be written (and probably more than one has been) on its causes and cures, but here's a brief note that may help explain this bugaboo of wooden hulls and in some places the wood inside fiberglass hulls. The rot comes from spores on the damp surface of wood that create a fungus which destroys the fibers and turns them into a spongy mass

Figure 3. Checking hull for dry rot and cracked planking. Knife shows split in strake to be repaired or replaced before boat goes back in the water.

with a distinctive stale, musty odor. In time, the wood crumbles into a powder. The rot is helped to grow and spread by the heat and condensation inside a hull that isn't properly ventilated—we'll get into this in Section 3—"The Maintenance Below".

If the paint appearance or condition of the wood doesn't show the location of rot, use a knife to probe suspected places for a spongy condition—tapping with a hammer will also help to detect it. When you find rot, the best cure is prompt surgery of the damaged area and replacement with new wood. In some cases, one of the chemical treatments that replace the rot with a self-hardening material may help.

PAINTING

On the topsides where the old paint is still good, and after you've cleaned it and made any repairs, all it may need is a light sanding before putting on a fresh coat. Flaking, blisters and heavy chalking usually call for stripping down to the wood. Use successive coats of paint remover to soften up the old finish so it can be taken off with a putty knife or scraper. Clean off any residue left from the remover with a solvent and sand lightly. A primer that's compatible with the paint should be used to prepare new wood. The Paint Chart at the end of this section will help in picking a finish for the top-sides.

As for the bottom, make sure it's thoroughly dry, sanded smooth and any damages fixed and primed. Pick one of the antifouling paints compatible with the old finish. Here again the Paint Chart will help. Follow the directions on the can for application, priming and thinning. Lay on a smooth even coat of the new paint—the roller method we outlined will speed up the work. Be careful though, to brush around the underwater hardware, zinc anodes, transducers, ground plates, etc., or you may affect their operation. A tip: If you're laying up a wooden boat for storage, some pros recommend giving the bottom a light coat of paint to keep the wood from shrinking and the caulking from drying out. This may also be necessary for wet storage, which we'll get into later in the book.

Aluminum Hulls

The alloys used in hulls today are designed for marine service and are basically corrosion-resistant. Most builders also give the metal a chemical treatment before painting that further helps to prevent corrosion in salt water. However, there is always the danger of galvanic corrosion which can attack and weaken the metal. We'll go into its causes and cures later in this section.

Figure 4. Bottom painting with a roller speeds job and lays on a smooth, even coat. Some antifouling paints are applied just before boat goes in water.

CLEANING

Because of the hardness of the metal, this work is a bit different from cleaning fiberglass or wood. The simplest way to clean aluminum is to wash it using a stiff brush and detergent or non-alkaline cleaner, followed by hosing. Another is the mechanical method, using bronze wool or wire brushing followed by a clear rinse. Chemical treatment, applying chromic or phosphoric acid, is a third route. New aluminum needs cleaning to remove the oil and mill scale from rolling and the surface must be etched slightly to bond the paint coating. On a rough surface—old paint, corrosion, patching, repairs, etc.—the metal must be thoroughly cleaned before painting. Regardless of how it is cleaned, the metal should be primed before painting—zinc chromate is commonly used. Any signs of corrosion, usually a white powder on the surface, that show up in the cleaning should be taken down to the bare metal, primed and painted.

PATCHING

Small dents, cracks and holes can be filled with an aluminum-base epoxy filler then sanded and primed. Larger dents can often be taken out with a rubber hammer, rolling them out like car fenders. Where some of the fastenings on a riveted hull have worked loose from vibration, use a backup block and ball-peen hammer to tighten them. When they've worked out completely, use a pop-rivet gun to put in replacements.

REPAIRING BREAKS AND HOLES

When these are too big for filling or where the metal is broken or cracked clean through, cover the damage with an aluminum patch. Cut a piece from an aluminum sheet slightly larger than the shape of the area and bend it to match the outside of the hull. Tape it in place over the hole or break while you drill holes around the circumference. Take off the patch and lay a coating of sealant on its hullside. Tape it back into place then use a pop-rivet gun in the holes to fasten it down. Grind down the edges of the patch to a slight bevel, fill the joint with epoxy filler and sand the whole area to blend with the surface. Follow with prime and paint.

TOPSIDES PAINTING

Where the old paint is in good condition with a smooth, clean surface, you may be able to lay a new coat over it with no further preparation. Just make sure the new paint is compatible with the old coating. Again, the Paint Chart at the end of this section will help you make a choice. If the old finish is gone, it may be best to strip it using a paint remover; but make sure the chemicals in it won't react with the aluminum—check the manufacturer's instructions on this. Where the surface is rough, wire brushing may be necessary after the residue from the paint remover has been taken off with a solvent. Follow this up with a non-scaling primer before applying the paint. Give the boot top the same treatment we outlined earlier for fiberglass and wooden hulls.

BOTTOM PAINTING

Here again if the cleaning and sanding you did after haulout left the old paint in good condition you're ahead of the game. Choosing an antifouling paint for aluminum is trickier than picking one for wood or fiberglass because some of the paints with cuprous oxide can produce galvanic corrosion of the metal. To avoid this, use a bottom paint with an organic toxicant instead of one with a copper base. The TBTO (Tributyltin Oxide) and TBTF (Tributyltin Fluoride) antifouling paints have organic toxicants and can be used on aluminum. Another type of bottom paint uses tin as a toxicant which also doesn't affect the metal.

Steel Hulls

The critical part of their maintenance is to prevent corrosion from both oxidation and galvanic action on the metal hull—inside and out. The amount of maintenance required depends to some degree on how well the metal was originally prepared for painting. This involves removing the mill scale from rolling the metal and the proper chemical treatment—priming with a chemical etch before painting. If both of these were done right and the paint coating kept up, a steel hull will normally give good service for many years.

CLEANING

After the initial washdown, go over any stubborn places with detergent and an abrasive cleaner. Localized spots where the paint coating has been broken and the rust is bleeding through should be sanded down to the bare metal, primed with zinc chromate, then painted immediately. *Don't let the bare metal stay exposed or it will quickly oxidize.* When the old paint has broken down over wide areas and a thick coating of rust has formed, the only way to remove it quickly and cleanly is to use sandblasting, which is best done by professionals using specialized equipment.

PATCHING AND REPAIRS

Small surface dents, cracks and nicks should be taken down to the bare metal, primed and filled with trowel cement or, better still, a metal-base epoxy filler. Use prime again over the repairs, sand smooth and paint. Large damage areas, where the steel has been bent, cracked or even punctured, call for the skills of a professional repairer. In some cases, the damage may require cutting out a section of plating with a torch and welding in a new piece. Before any painting is done, make sure the new steel is properly treated and primed.

TOPSIDES PAINTING

Here again if the old finish is in good shape, a light sanding may be all you need do before laying on a fresh coating. Any rust spots in the topsides should be treated as outlined before, paying special attention to priming the bare metal to get good adhesion. As a general rule, the epoxy paints are preferable for a steel hull because they bond well, are tough, and resist weathering. The Paint Chart at the end of this section will help you pick a finish, but again, make sure it is compatible with the old one.

BOTTOM PAINTING

The important thing to remember in doing this is to use an antifouling paint that will not produce galvanic corrosion of the steel hull. Cuprous-oxide paints should not be used. Instead, use a paint with tin as the inhibitor or an organic one like the TBTO or TBTF coatings we suggested earlier for bottom paints on aluminum.

Electrolysis and Galvanic Corrosion

So far, the hull care we've covered has involved protecting it from deterioration caused by weather or the sea, using some form of covering to do the job. And yet, there is another enemy that like a thief in the night, silent and unseen, can cause as much damage as the elements and can't be prevented by use of a protective material. This is the corrosion of metal in a hull by electrolysis or by galvanic action.

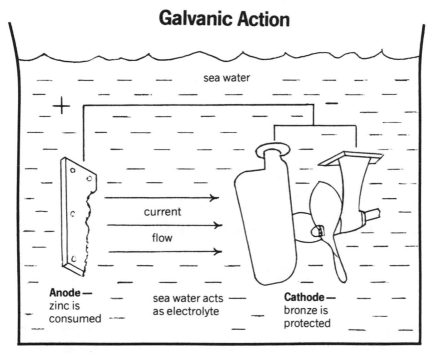

Galvanic Action

sea water

+

current

flow

Anode— zinc is consumed

sea water acts as electrolyte

Cathode— bronze is protected

Figure 5. How a zinc anode protects underwater hardware from galvanic corrosion, which happens when two different metals are in sea water, causing an electric current to flow between them.

While both are basically electro-chemical reactions, the corrosion by electrolysis happens when an electric current in a solution (in the case of a boat, the salt water around it) turns one of the metals into an anode and another into a cathode. The reaction corrodes the anode metal and breaks it down, and that is why zinc anodes are used for protection. The current that creates the electrolysis may come from inside the boat, as in leakage from the electrical system, or from an improperly connected grounding system. It can also come from an external source, such as a shoreside power connection or even the electrical systems of neighboring boats.

The galvanic action that causes corrosion is also an electro-chemical process occurring when different metals in a solution (again, the salt water around the boat) produce their own electric current by making one metal the anode and another the cathode. Here again the anode metal is corroded and broken down. The best example of a useful galvanic action is that in a storage battery where it generates direct current; but in the case of the metals in a boat hull, the action can be corrosive and harmful.

The factor that determines the resistance of metals to corrosion by galvanic action is their potential to form an anode (those with a high potential) or a cathode (those with a low potential). The relative corrosion potentials of metals used in marine service are shown in the following table. The metals are arranged in numbered groups and any two metals in the same group can generally be used together with little or no corrosion occurring. Copper and Monel, for example, will usually not corrode when they are in contact. But metals from different groups, when used together, will corrode. To take an example, aluminum (near the top of the table) will corrode when used with copper (lower down in the table). The farther apart the metals are in the table the greater the chance for corrosion. Galvanized steel (with a high potential) will corrode in contact with stainless steel (18-8) (passive) with a lower potential, because the galvanic action will be greater.

GALVANIC SERIES OF METALS
Corrosion Potentials in Sea Water

High Potential to Corrosion (Forms Anode)	1	Magnesium Magnesium Alloys
	2	Zinc
	3	Aluminum
	4	Cadmium
	5	Galvanized Steel Or Iron Cast Iron
	6	Chromium Iron (active)
	7	Stainless Steel (18-8) (active)
	8	Lead-Tin Solders Lead Tin
	9	Nickel (active)
	10	Brasses Copper Bronzes Copper-Nickel Alloys Titanium Monel
	11	Nickel (passive)
Low Potential to Corrosion (Forms Cathode)	12	Chromium Iron (passive) Stainless Steel (passive)

MINIMIZING ELECTROLYSIS AND GALVANIC ACTION

There are several ways to control corrosion from both actions—some simple, others more complex. The first step is to check the electrical circuits aboard, including the battery, for any current leakage. An electrician can eliminate this for you. It is also important to have all large metal parts such as tanks, fuel-filler pipes, seacocks, etc. connected to the boat's bonding system and, in turn, to the engine block. This will also prevent accidental sparks that could cause gas fumes to explode in the bilge.

USE OF ZINC PLATES AND COLLARS

With this method, the zincs are fastened to the rudders, bolted around shafts, or to the hull to protect the underwater hardware from galvanic corrosion. In time, the zincs will be consumed and should be replaced. You can also get the same protection by bonding all the underwater parts and the engine together then using one "master" zinc anode. A variation on this method is to monitor the current produced by the zinc, using a solid-state controller and meters inside the hull, so it counteracts any corrosion of the other metals and only the zinc is eaten away.

ELECTRONIC PROTECTION SYSTEMS

These are more elaborate methods that use DC current from the boat's 12-volt system with an electronic device and a master zinc anode to neutralize and automatically control any galvanic corrosion. While not as complex as these systems, you can also use a reverse-polarity indicator on a shore-power cable to warn you if the grounding connector is producing galvanic corrosion. There is also a transformer to isolate the boat's electrical system from any connection with the metals ashore or the systems of other boats sharing the same power line.

SEPARATING DISSIMILAR METALS

Separation by non-metallic materials is the way to prevent galvanic corrosion between metals with a big difference in potentials as shown in the above table. For example, the underwater hardware on a metal hull (such as struts and rudders, usually made of bronze) should be separated from the hull with plastic spacers. Most builders try to use metals close together in the galvanic series to avoid this. This type

Figure 6. Zinc anodes on rudders and shafts prevent galvanic corrosion and should be replaced when deteriorated.

of corrosion can also occur on the bottoms of metal hulls when an antifouling paint with a metallic inhibitor is used. To prevent galvanic corrosion, a barrier coating should first be applied. Galvanic corrosion can also take place between dissimilar metals on glass or wooden hulls unless they are separated by an insulating material.

ABOVE-DECK GALVANIC CORROSION

While underwater hardware is usually thought of as the most likely place for corrosion of this kind, it can also attack metal above decks where the salt-laden air acts as the "solution" to produce galvanic action. For this reason, all fittings on deck and aloft for both power- and sailboats should be checked regularly for signs of corrosion. We'll cover this in the next section.

UNDERWATER HARDWARE

While your boat is hauled, go over this hardware, checking for damage and the corrosion just described. Begin with the rudders: Any cracks in the metal, dry rot under the fittings on a wooden hull? Do the props next: Any bent or broken blades? If so, pull the wheels for reconditioning or replacement. Check the struts for wear in the bearings, loose fastenings to the hull. Have someone work the steering controls while you check the rudders for excess play in cables or linkage. Do the same thing on the trim tabs. Go over the ground plate and depthsounder transducer: Fastenings tight; any dry rot under them? Check the zincs, anodes, collars, plates, etc. for deterioration. Remember, they're for protection, so don't be chintzy about replacing them.

THROUGH-HULL FITTINGS, SEACOCKS AND INLETS

These are important to the smooth operation of equipment below decks, so check them out while you're working on the hull. Here again, look for galvanic corrosion, loose fastenings, cracked metal. Clean off the debris from all the strainers on the water intakes.

CHAINPLATES AND BACKSTAY FITTINGS

Where these are outside the hull, make them a part of your overall hardware inspection. Look for corrosion and cracks in the metal from the stress on shrouds and stays. If the cracks are deep enough to weaken the plate, have it replaced by a professional. Any loose fastenings should be tightened or, if the holes are worn, replaced by larger size bolts. Since the chainplates on fiberglass hulls are usually fastened inside to gussets or bulkheads, we'll cover these in Section 3, "The Maintenance Below."

RUB STRAKES AND GUNWALE GUARDS

These can take a beating during the season and your annual maintenance should include them. Where the rub strakes are wood and have a metal cap, look for loose fastenings and corrosion at the butt ends. Check, too, between the facing, the strake and wooden hull for signs of dry rot. Gunwale guards of aluminum with a vinyl-moulding insert also need care. If the vinyl has popped out in some places, squeeze it back in with a putty knife or rubber hammer. Long stretches of this trouble may mean it's lost its bounce, so the whole insert should be replaced, but let a pro do it.

Outside Sterndrive Maintenance

Along with its advantages, a little more upkeep is needed on the drive unit outside the hull than on a regular inboard. If you follow the service manual though, the maintenance is usually pretty straightforward, and should be done at the

Figure 7. Gunwale guards: A) split pipe on steel and aluminum hulls, B) vinyl guard on small wood and fiberglass boats, C) aluminum with vinyl insert on fiberglass hulls, D) wooden rub strake with metal facing on heavy hulls.

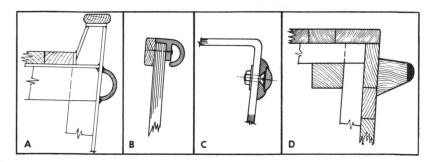

start of the season and about every 50 hours of running time thereafter.

The maintenance of the sterndrive inside the hull is covered in the next section, but here is what the upkeep of the outside drive unit usually involves. It will vary depending on the manufacturer, so use his manual for the details:

1. Clean the entire outside drive unit of any marine growth, rust and grease, then check for any loose or damaged parts which need to be fixed or replaced.
2. Drain the oil in the gear case—some manufacturers have separate systems for the upper and lower sections. Check the color of the oil for water contamination—the oil usually turns a light brown. Any signs of this can mean a leaking seal or cracked housing—in either case, have the dealer or yard mechanic check and repair. If there are no signs of leaks, refill the case (or parts of it) with the recommended lubricant.
3. Lubricate all the outside pivot points and linkages. If any fittings won't take grease, clean them out and put in fresh lubricant with a hand gun.
4. Go over all the cooling-water passages you can get at; use a wire to loosen any deposits, then vacuum them out. Take off any removable inlet screens and clean them. Wrap up the job by flushing out the entire unit, using a hose adaptor if needed.
5. On power trim systems, check the hydraulic connections for tightness. To work smoothly, the cylinder shafts should be clean and shiny. Take off any dirt and rust with fine emery cloth and lubricate them.
6. Inspect the transom boot and all external rubber parts for brittleness, cracks and wear. Replace any that need it.
7. Before you remove the propeller, play it safe by taking the key out of the ignition. Check the wheel for nicks and bent blades. You can take out small nicks with a file, but anything beyond this needs the work of a pro.
8. With the prop off, check the zinc collar under it and any others on the outside drive unit to see if they've been consumed—if so, replace with new zincs.

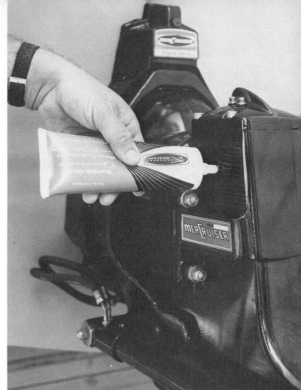

Figure 8. Refilling upper gear case of sterndrive with lubricant. Sealing gaskets must be in good condition to prevent water entering case and damaging gear train.

Figure 9. Lubricating shaft on sterndrive. Water-resistant grease makes it easier to remove prop in an emergency.

9. Before you replace the prop, coat the spline with water-resistant grease so you can get it off in an emergency.
10. To prevent galvanic action and marine growth from building up on the drive unit, spray on a coat of paint for this purpose.

Paints and Painting

At the beginning of this section, we said care of the hull was the most important part of a maintenance program and by now, your work on it should be almost finished. But all the time and effort that went into it won't mean much unless you protect the surfaces from the weather and the sea with a coating of paint. And the same thing holds true for surfaces above the deck and also those below, which we'll get into in later sections.

But for now, here are some of the basic points in painting that you can use to good advantage in getting durable finishes that will protect your pride and joy:

PREPARATION

Most pros will tell you that a painting job really begins with the first scraping and sanding of the old finish. Unless the surface is in good condition *before* you paint, you'll never get the protection the manufacturer has built into it. Where the old finish is smooth and hard, all it may need is a light sanding. If it is not, you may have to strip it with paint remover and solvent. If it needs sanding, choose the right grit size and buy production paper—it cuts faster and lasts longer.

CHOOSING A PAINT

The chart of Marine Paint Families at the end of this section will help you do this. It lists the major marine finishes by their chemical bases, where to use them and their pros and cons. When you pick one of the finishes, think of the family as a *complete chemical system* with its own primer or sealer, thinner and finish coating—all formulated to work together and produce a durable coating. Don't try to mix the thinner from one family with the finish coating from another; they may not be compatible and you can ruin the job.

USING THE RIGHT PAINTING TOOLS

These are what brushes and rollers really are, and the old rule of using good tools for a good job applies to painting. Buy good brushes—the extra dollars for "professional quality" really pay off. Make sure the bristles are compatible with the paint you're using—nylon, for example, is attacked by some epoxies. And give your brushes tender loving care. Clean them after each use and hang them up to dry so the bristles won't curl. Varnish brushes need special care.

READ THE CAN

It almost seems as though this should be stencilled in red letters on every lid—it's that important to a good paint job. The manufacturer went to a lot of trouble to give you the kind of instructions to ensure a long-lasting finish, so follow his advice on surface preparation, mixing, thinning, applying, drying time, etc.—the works. Most states require the label also list the ingredients and warn if any are toxic.

USE A COMPATIBLE FINISH

Before you apply any paint, make sure it will work on the old finish. Any doubts, test a small area first to make sure it dries to a hard smooth coating. If it blisters and dissolves the old paint, you're in the wrong ballpark, so try another one of the families on the Paint Chart. Some owners save the cans from the last season (even empty ones) and grease-paint the date they used them. This way they can match the new paint to the old when the new season rolls around.

NONSKID FINISH

In painting housetops and decks, there may be areas where it's important to have sure footing for handling sails or an-

Figure 10. Painting centerboard trunk on small sailboats using skinny roller. Flat stick covered with rag will also do the job.

chor tackle. Since some painted surfaces are quite slippery when wet, you can get a nonskid surface by mixing in a can of special powder or granules most marine-supply houses carry. The amount used determines the degree of roughness and there are instructions on the can.

MATCHING COLORS

This is a tricky job even for professional painters since any coating weathers and also the color may vary slightly from one batch to another in the manufacturer's plant. Where the color match is important, try to bring a sample of the old color with you and if you have any doubts before using the new paint, try it out first in a small, inconspicuous spot. Your dealer may be able to change the formula to improve the match.

VARNISHING

There's no question brightwork can add to the beauty of a boat by bringing out the natural color of the wood, but it takes time and patience to do a good varnishing job. Surface preparation with bleaching and restaining, if necessary, are important and so are outside conditions. Try to pick a clear, warm, dry day with no wind to blow dust over the new coating. Use a good brush and allow ample time to get a hard, tough coating. Several coats of varnish are often better than trying to lay on a thick one.

HOW MUCH PAINT WILL YOU NEED?

The table below shows one manufacturer's estimates of the paint needed to put two coats on the major areas of different types and sizes of boats. The figures are for applying two coats on surfaces already painted—for bare ones, double the quantities. It's better to buy too much paint than too little—any surplus can always be used for touchup later.

MARINE PAINT FAMILIES
How to Use Them, Where and Why

FAMILY BY CHEMICAL BASE	WHERE TO USE	PROS	CONS	OTHER INFORMATION
Alkyd-Oil	Almost everywhere above the waterline—topsides, decks, cabins and housetops. On fiberglass, in some places, wood and metal.	Good for all-around marine use. Ready-mixed in single cans. Wide color range. Quick drying time. Relatively low cost.	Softer than epoxies and urethanes. Not suitable for some fiberglass surfaces because of poor bond.	Alkyds are often modified with other chemicals like acrylics, phenols and silicones for better moisture resistance and to improve other properties.
Antifouling Metallic Toxicants	Bottoms of fiberglass and wooden hulls. (Use TBTO & TBTF paints on metal hulls.)	Toxicants, usually cuprous-oxide or bronze flakes which inhibit and kill marine growth. Slow-drying, easy to apply one-part packaging.	Fumes may be toxic, also dust from sanding. Mask and goggles are musts. Needs frequent stirring.	Don't use on aluminum and steel hulls as metallic-toxicants can cause galvanic corrosion unless a barrier paint is used first.
Vinyls (Polyvinyl-chloride Base)	Mostly as antifouling bottom paint but also on cabin sides and tops, decks.	Rubber-like qualities—flexible, resist abrasion, chemicals and weather. Good adhesion. Ideal for metal surfaces.	Poor adhesion on fiberglass. Hard to apply. Not compatible with most other paint families.	Often used as a racing finish on bottoms of small boats that are trailered.

Epoxies	Excellent above the waterline on steel hulls, also on fiberglass where it forms a chemical bond.	Hard and tough, high gloss, resistant to abrasion and chemicals. Come in one- and two-part cans.	High viscosity makes them harder to brush. Tend to chalk, not good for topsides affected by sunlight. Relatively expensive. Not suitable over antifouling paints.	Use only natural bristle brushes, the resins in epoxies will attack nylon. Slightly toxic, use only in well-ventilated areas. Apply only above 70 degrees.
Polyurethanes	Topside areas, especially where weathering is a factor. Excellent for exposed brightwork in varnish formulations.	Excellent adhesion, forms hard, tough coating that resists traffic and sunlight. Whites are non-yellowing. Come in one- and two-part systems.	More costly. Require care in application. Two-part systems should follow manufacturer's instructions exactly.	Apply in warm temperatures in a dust-free atmosphere.
TBTO (Tributyltin Oxide) TBTF (Tributyltin Fluoride) Antifouling Paints	On fiberglass and metal hull bottoms: TBTO can also be used on wooden hulls.	Good on aluminum and steel because the non-metallic toxicants won't cause galvanic corrosion of the metal.	Relatively expensive. Highly toxic.	Both TBTO and TBTF go on well over vinyl and cuprous-oxide paints on wood and fiberglass hulls. Since the antifouling ingredients in TBTO & TBTF paints don't dry out they are good for boats trailered or stored between uses.

ESTIMATED PAINT NEEDS
(For two coats on old paint—double amounts on bare surfaces)

TYPE	SIZE	TOPSIDES	BOTTOM	WATERLINE	DECK	VARNISH	INTERIOR	ENGINE
Dinghy	10'	1 Pt.	1 Pt.	—	—	1½ Qts.	—	—
Rowboat	14'	1 Qt.	1 Qt.	—	—	—	—	—
Outboard	14'	1 Qt.	1 Qt.	—	1 Pt.	1 Qt.	—	½ Pt.
Runabout	18'	2 Qts.	2 Qts.	½ Pt.	1 Qt.	1 Pt.	—	½ Pt. or 16 oz. Spray
Runabout	24'	2 Qts.	3 Qts.	½ Pt.	1 Qt.	1½ Qts.	—	1 Pt. or 16 oz. Spray
Utility	24'	2 Qts.	3 Qts.	½ Pt.	1 Qt.	1 Qt.	—	1 Pt. or 16 oz. Spray
Cruiser	25'	2 Qts.	3 Qts.	1 Pt.	1½ Qts.	1½ Qts.	2 Qts.	1 Pt. or 16 oz. Spray
Cruiser	32'	1 Gal.	1½ Gals.	1 Pt.	2 Qts.	2 Qts.	2 Qts.	1 Pt. or 16 oz. Spray
Cruiser	40'	2½ Gals.	2 Gals.	1 Pt.	1½ Gals.	1 Gal.	1 Gal.	1 Qt. or 2 16 oz. Spray
Yacht	60'	4 Gals.	5 Gals.	1 Qt.	3½ Gals.	2½ Gals.	3 Gals.	1½ Qts. or 2 16 oz. Spray

(Table: International Paint Company, Inc.)

2. Above-Deck Care

With most of the work done on the outside of the hull, you can then move aboard and begin the spruceup above decks. Here the nature of the upkeep changes, with less work on materials and more to be done on equipment. On a sailboat, the spars and rigging, deck fittings and winches, etc.; on powerboats, some rigging, plus instruments and controls on the flying bridge, deck hardware, etc. Both power and sail may need work on cabins and deckhouses, covers and awnings, and all the other equipment there, right down to the maintenance of the deck itself.

To simplify the topside work after the preliminary jobs are done, we've divided it into the specialized care normally done on sailboats, on powerboats, and the upkeep chores they both share.

Masthead-to-Deck Washdown

We mentioned this before in the previous section on hull care but if you've skipped it or decided to begin your annual maintenance on the topsides, the washdown should be a starter. The seagull mess is probably hardest to remove, especially from canvas, rigging and parts of the deck gear. Soaking with a detergent and a working over with a stiff brush will help get off the gop. Use an abrasive scrubber like ScotchBrite on the stubborn spots and the inevitable scuff marks on heavy-traffic areas on deck.

Topside Cleaning and Repairs

We also covered this in the hull-care section, but it's worth repeating especially in the case of fiberglass where you can damage the gel coat if the cleaning isn't done carefully. Most goofs in painted wooden and metal surfaces can be covered with a new coating, but repairing gel-coat damage is tricky. You can get repair kits for the job from marine-supply stores and catalog houses. If a lot of fiberglass repair work is needed, buy larger quantities of resin, cloth and mat separately—it's cheaper than kits. Epoxy putties are harder to work with than polyester in fixing surface damage but they have more strength and durability.

In repairing surface damages on wood, use a trowelling compound, followed by sanding, priming and painting. On aluminum and steel, make sure you remove the corrosion and rust down to bare metal, then prime with zinc chromate before filling with a metal-base epoxy. Sand the spot, prime again and paint.

Since repair of decks varies for fiberglass, planked wood, canvas-covered, metal, etc., we'll go into detail on their upkeep later in this section.

Sailboat Maintenance Above Deck

Outside of the hull, everything topsides on your boat—sails, spars, rigging, winches, etc.—probably represents the largest single investment you have in it. And the same equipment is as vulnerable to attack by the elements and corrosion. As a result, topsides upkeep on a sailboat is more complex than on a powerboat and requires a more regular and detailed maintenance program.

CARING FOR SAILS

Let's begin with the biggest cost item—your sails. With proper care most of the Dacron used today should last for a number of years—longer if you're fussy. Here are some of the points to keep in mind in caring for them.

Repairs. Well-done stitching, darning and patching will fix most minor rips and tears from normal wear without affecting performance or the life of the sail. When a tear develops, get the sail down pronto and don't use it until it's fixed.

On-the-spot repairs can be made with a kit sold by marine-supply stores—they also sell pressure-sensitive repair tape

Figure 11. Covers protect sails stored on spars from weather and dirt. Torn seam needs repair to keep out moisture.

that just presses on. For more durable repairs, use the kit that usually comes with Dacron thread, needles (in some cases a lockstitch awl), and a wooden or stainless fid. You can get the material for patches from a sailmaker's scrap bin—usually for the asking. A sailmaker's palm with a built-in thimble socket will make stitching of heavy fabric easier. With a little experience, you can darn, resew seams, fix batten pockets and do other repairs. On torn-out grommets, use a repair kit that comes with dies, or pliers, and an assortment of grommets. Do-it-yourself repairs can save money, but know the limit of your skill—if the job looks like it's beyond it, take it to a sailmaker.

Chafing and Wear. This is most apt to happen at the points of greatest strain—around batten pockets, tack points, clews and headboards, etc. When the wear comes from chafing on standing rigging, find the culprit and insulate the spot with chafing tape that comes by the roll. You can also use baggywrinkle to prevent chafing if you don't mind its fuzzy looks.

Cleaning. The sail wardrobe on most boats takes a beating not only from dirt and normal usage, but from air pollution almost everywhere today—especially in waters around big cities. Where the dirt hasn't been ground into the fabric or stained by pollution, you can usually clean it yourself. Spread the sail out on a flat area and use a mild detergent and scrub brush (with care) on stubborn spots, then hose off the dirt. Do the job on a clear, warm day with enough of a breeze so the fabric will blow a bit and take out the wrinkles when hung by the leech to dry. When sails are badly stained and haven't been cleaned for some time, let a sailmaker do a professional cleaning job on them. Also have him take out any grease or dirt a detergent won't dissolve—don't try it yourself with dry-cleaning fluid or acetone, the reaction with Dacron can be a disaster.

MASTS AND SPARS

When your boat is hauled for annual maintenance and the yard has unstepped the mast, it's a lot easier to do any upkeep on the spars on the ground than to tackle it from a bosn's chair aloft. Whichever way, start by giving aluminum spars an in-depth check for stress cracks and corrosion—the latter often shows up as a white powder on the surface. Other spots are where the anodizing has worn away.

If there are deep cracks in the welds or stress cracks in the metal, have a rigger check the mast to make sure it hasn't been weakened. Shallow cracks can be filled, sanded and covered with an epoxy coating. If possible, take off any cleats and winches mounted on the spar, checking for corrosion beneath them, and for signs of wear on the fastenings (enlarged holes). And take a look at the sail track and its fastenings.

Alloy spars and their fittings can be corroded by the galvanic action we described in the previous section. This is most likely to occur where dissimilar metals are in contact —for example, a bronze halyard winch on an aluminum mast. To prevent corrosion, the two metals should be insulated with a barrier of plastic.

Check all alloy spars, too, in places where fittings like outhauls, tangs, etc. are mounted to make sure the holes for fastenings haven't become enlarged. Begin your inspection at the masthead, checking the sheaves for wear, then work your way down. Look over the spreaders for splits in the wood and the fittings, on the mast for cracks and corrosion. While you're there, have someone turn on the spreader lights to make sure they're okay.

While you're checking out an alloy mast, don't overlook the foot which is often stepped on a steel shoe in the bilge and can be corroded by salt water. Take off any rust or corrosion on the foot or step by wire-brushing, prime the steel with zinc chromate, the aluminum with a non-scaling primer, then give them both a coat of epoxy.

Wooden spars and the fittings mounted on them should be given the same treatment as alloy ones. Look again for corrosion or cracks in the fittings, for loose fastenings and for any signs of dry rot or structural weakness in the wood. If you find any of these troubles, take prompt action to remedy them. After it's done, refinish the wood and replace any fittings you removed.

Before you finish the work on the mast, and while it's still on the ground, pull out the halyards that run inside and check them for signs of wear. They're out of sight but shouldn't be out of mind. Replace any worn lines before the mast is stepped back in the boat.

STANDING RIGGING

This needs special attention in any maintenance program due to stress on it under sail and exposure to salt spray which, here again, can cause galvanic corrosion of the metal. If you didn't do it in the overall washdown, get at the standing rigging now, cleaning off all salt and grime. Give the wire an inch-by-inch inspection looking for cracks, wear and corrosion. Most stainless steel will last for a number of years with little care other than routine cleaning. The galvanized wire can be a problem where the zinc coating has worn off exposing the steel to rust. Sand this off, prime the spots with zinc chromate and coat with a metallic epoxy paint. Watch out for "fishhooks"—broken strands that can cut hands and rip sails. Cut these off and bind the broken strands with waterproof tape. A string of fishhooks in a stretch of wire means it's probably gone to pot and should be replaced.

Turnbuckles on standing rigging also need upkeep. Back off the barrels and look for damaged threads or worn toggle pins. If the turnbuckles look okay, grease them and run the barrels back up.

Cotterpins in fittings can also be a source of trouble when the ends aren't bent over right and can injure hands and damage sails. The solution here is to bind them with tape or slide a length of plastic tube over the whole business, turnbuckle and toggle, right down to the top of the chainplate.

RUNNING RIGGING

Give all the blocks and tackle in this a close check for cracks in the cheeks, worn grooves that can fray the lines. Replace any damaged ones before the next season. Also give the furling or roller-reefing gear an inspection for corrosion or cracked metal in the hardware. Now is the time to fix or refit, not when you're under sail and something breaks down.

Wire and Cordage. Finish the upkeep on the running rigging by going over all the wire and cordage—especially at stress points where it goes through a block or over a sheave. If you haven't already checked the halyards inside the mast as suggested earlier, put them on your work list if the spar is still on the ground.

It's a good idea to check all sheets before the season begins, looking for chafe and wear at the lead ends. They can be turned end for end, but the leads must also be checked to make sure there's no foulup there.

Most of the cordage in running rigging today is nylon or Dacron requiring little maintenance other than an occasional washing in fresh water to get out the salt. The lines will deteriorate a bit if they're left out in the sun but that will take a long time to happen. Any splices in cordage, especially those in anchor rodes and dock lines get a lot of stress in heavy weather, so make sure they're in good condition. Replace any splices that look weak when you handle the lines or use new ones completely.

SERVICING WINCHES

For most sailboat owners, their investment in winches is often a major one because the original inventory has probably been changed to improve sail-handling performance. This reason and the fact they must be depended on completely in an emergency should get them top priority on your work list.

In servicing winches, it is important to remember that a good winch for its original cost will do more work with fewer breakdowns than almost any other piece of equipment on board, *if it is properly maintained.* Here is what this usually involves for most winches:

1. Don't Let the Works Scare You. Your first reaction when you take off the drum may be "My God, look at all the

parts inside!" But don't panic, they're not as complex as they look. By doing the servicing slowly and carefully, and following the manufacturer's manual, you should be able to do the work short of any major repairs that require a pro. The drawing of a typical winch's construction should help clear up any mystery of what happens when you turn the crank.

2. Dismantling and Cleaning. Do this at least once a season—more often, if you sail year-round. Salt spray and pollution will get inside and gum up the works. Before you start the cleaning job, get out the service manual and keep it handy. Use a bucket to keep the parts in so they don't get lost. Take off the drum slowly and carefully so the pawls which are spring-loaded don't pop out. Most of the time there'll be nothing broken inside. Dismantle the works, remembering how the parts fit together, then clean them with a solvent the manufacturer recommends.

3. Inspect All the Parts. As you clean them, check for any cracks or signs of wear in the gear teeth, pawls, rachet or shaft. If the winch bucked or skipped during the season, it may be a sign of wear or broken parts. On reel-halyard winches, look at the drum for scoring and cracks where the brake band rides. When you're satisfied the parts are okay, lubricate them with whatever the manufacturer specifies. Don't get any grease on the pawls or springs, or the brake bands of halyard winches. Assemble the winch, and using the service manual, follow any drawing of the mechanism in it.

4. Check the Winch Mounting. Look at the base and make sure the drain holes are free—bedding compound sometimes clogs them. Most winch manufacturers will tell you that water trapped inside is one of the major causes of damage, such as a broken rachet.

5. Keep a Spare-Parts Kit Aboard. The small cost of these is well worth it. Most come in a handy waterproof case with replacements for the parts most apt to break. Without a kit, at least have a spare bearing, pawls, springs and a snap ring for each winch you have on board.

Figure 12a. Greasing spindle of a two-speed winch. Old lubricant and dirt are first removed with solvent.

Figure 12b. Cleaning roller bearings of a self-tailing winch. Stripper arm is in left foreground.

Figure 12c. Oiling pawls of a two-speed sheet winch. Gears are greased before reassembly.

6. Use Covers. To help keep winches in good condition, always keep them covered when not in use during the season. Use boots or other forms of protection. In a pinch, small plastic buckets like the kids use at a beach will do the trick. Covers are also a must when you lay up the boat for storage.

7. Winch Handles. These will take quite a beating, in fact their mortality rate depends more on their going over the side than breaking in service. Handles require some care though—oiling at the grips, and if you have ratchet types, cleaning and lubrication. Make sure your handles are kept handy to the winches and tight in a seaway— the flexible PVC holsters from marine supply stores will take most standard-size handles.

DECK FITTINGS AND HARDWARE

These require preventive maintenance at least once during the season. Your first job is to make sure the fastenings are tight. Most builders through-bolt all deck hardware with backing or doubler blocks underneath. If they've been skipped in some places on your boat, you can install them yourself. Oil all moving parts on deck fittings, as well as the blocks there, including the parts on cam cleats.

Next, give all deck hardware a good inspection looking for cracks and corrosion—two of the most likely spots are at chainplates going through the deck and plates for snatch and turning blocks. On a wooden hull, test around the fittings for any signs of dry rot caused by water lodging beneath them.

Here are some of the more common deck fittings that sometimes need a little special care:

Blocks. Check all these for cracks in the straps, cheeks or sheaves. If any show up, replace the blocks. Wooden sheaves particularly are apt to crack from moisture and swelling.

Slides. In addition to checking their fastenings, look for burrs and dents in the edges that can jam a traveller. Straighten the metal and smooth any rough spots with a file.

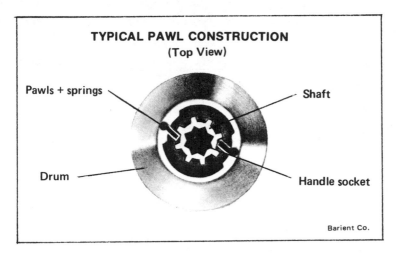

TYPICAL PAWL CONSTRUCTION
(Top View)

Pawls + springs

Shaft

Drum

Handle socket

Barient Co.

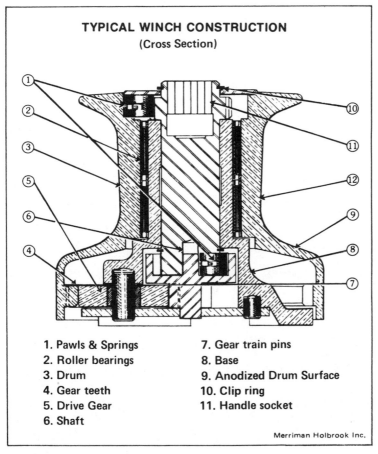

TYPICAL WINCH CONSTRUCTION
(Cross Section)

1. Pawls & Springs
2. Roller bearings
3. Drum
4. Gear teeth
5. Drive Gear
6. Shaft
7. Gear train pins
8. Base
9. Anodized Drum Surface
10. Clip ring
11. Handle socket

Merriman Holbrook Inc.

Figure 13.

Chocks and Fairleads. Here's where corrosion can roughen openings to fray lines and sheet leads. Use emery cloth to smooth the holes.

Pad Eyes. So small they may be overlooked but still important. Check for loose fastenings and cracks especially the eyes that hold spinnaker blocks and get a lot of strain.

ON-DECK MAST STEPS

Mountings like these, or in some cases tabernacles for lowering the mast flat, are other pieces of deck hardware that may need upkeep. Scan the alloy of the step for cracks or corrosion—anything serious calls for an expert's eye too, and if necessary rewelding or replacement. Tabernacles should get the same treatment, including any moving parts which should be lubricated.

MAST BOOT OR COLLARS

Where masts are stepped through the deck, the openings are likely places for leaks on all hulls and dry rot on wooden ones. To cover the wedges around the mast, there's usually a boot or collar of rubberized fabric that also seals the opening against water. In time, this can crack, so check and replace if needed. When you do it, tighten the wedges underneath it.

STANCHIONS, PULPITS AND LIFELINES

All these are important to the safety of the crew while handling sail in a seaway, or when the boat is heeled. Test each stanchion with the "wobble" method for loose fastenings, then check the deck plate for cracks. All fastenings should be tight and any cracked plates replaced. Give the pulpit the same test and treatment.

Lifelines are usually of stainless steel wire with a plastic covering that often cracks and peels at heavy traffic points. You can replace the bad sections with plastic tubing that comes slit for this purpose.

THE STEERING STATION ON SAILBOATS

The maintenance program above decks should include this with rudder and engine controls, compass, instruments and other hardware usually at the station. These usually need more upkeep than on a powerboat because of greater exposure to weather. Here's what the work at a station generally includes:

Steering Systems. For a rudder and tiller affair hung on the transom, maintenance is no problem. Make sure the pintles and gudgeons are tightly fastened; on a wooden hull, check for any evidence of dry rot.

Larger boats may have an inboard system with the rudder below the hull controlled by a shaft going through it. Here the topside fittings should be checked for loose fastenings, and bearing points should be lubricated. Turn the wheel over hard—any excess play can mean worn parts or linkage in the system. Care of the stuffing box at the bottom of the rudder stock will be covered in the next section.

The above-deck parts of a pedestal system are usually serviced by oiling the sheaves once a month during the season and lubricating the mechanism inside the pedestal at every other maintenance. A handgun can be used to grease fittings on the bearings there. Here again, spin the wheel over hard to find any excess play and worn linkage in the parts below deck. We'll cover these in the next section.

Some boats may have a rack and pinion system which controls the wheel through a gearing arrangement. You should grease the parts and shaft bearing in it.

Engine Controls. These are next on your work list. Make sure the throttle and clutch levers work smoothly with no signs of excess play in the linkages. We'll go into the upkeep of the below-deck parts in the next section. If you've had any leaks where the levers go through the cockpit floor, you can stop these by using rubber boots over them.

Instruments. There was a time when these were fairly sim-

Sailboat Steering—
Pedestal System

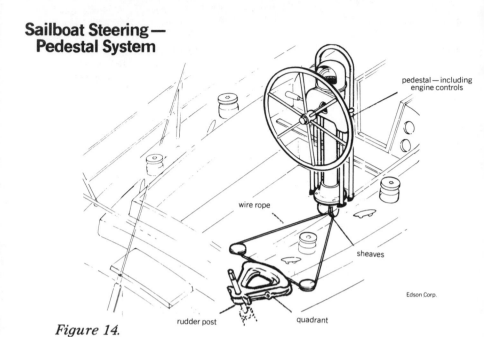

pedestal—including
engine controls

wire rope

sheaves

Edson Corp.

rudder post

quadrant

Figure 14.

Sailboat Steering—
Rack and Pinion System

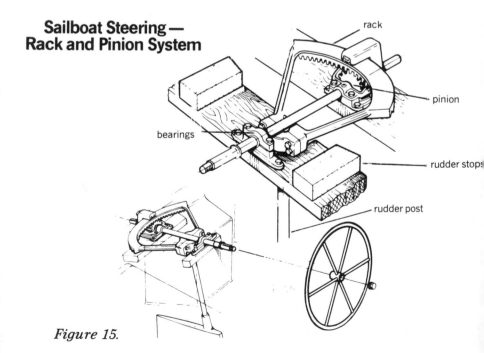

rack

pinion

bearings

rudder stops

rudder post

Figure 15.

ple at the helm station on a sailboat—usually the compass and, if it had an auxiliary, the engine controls. Today is the electronic age and it may have reached your boat in the form of instruments to monitor sailing performance. If any of these have developed gremlins during the season, take them to a specialist ashore for checking and repair.

How long since you've had the compass swung? You may have changed equipment around it that can throw off the compensation. If the answer is "yes", have it done again. And don't overlook the instruments on the engine panel; these are usually pretty foolproof, but an ammeter can be off and the oil pressure and temperature gauges can develop trouble at the block.

Powerboat Maintenance Above Deck

There's less fuss keeping up the topsides on a powerboat than on a sailboat. Most of the maintenance on a typical cruiser is straightforward work that's easily done. Here are the major items that should be on your "give-it-a-check" list:

DECK GEAR

Signal Mast. Begin at the top by testing the light, then work your way down looking for cracks if the mast is wood, corrosion if it's alloy. Any loose fastenings in the fittings that hold the stays or the plate or step that holds the mast on deck? Look for corrosion here too, if it's of alloy, dry rot if it's wood. Finally, take a hard look at the paint or varnish coating—does it need refinishing to perk up its appearance?

Searchlight. Where there's one mounted on the cabin top, see if the fastenings are tight. Remote-control lights sometimes develop leaks in the cabin top so check the mounting for these. Any moving parts that are exposed should be lubricated.

Antenna. Here's another piece of topside gear that can develop bugs during the season. Frying noises may mean corrosion on the contacts inside the lead-in connection. These should be kept clean with emery cloth, followed by a shot of anti-corrosive spray. Are there any loose fastenings in the mounting to swing down the whip—any parts corroded?

Handrails and Grabrails. Give these the "wobble" test to check for loose fastenings. Does the wood or alloy in the rails need refinishing? Any broken parts in the hardware at the boarding gate? Add work needed on these to your "nitty-gritty" job list.

Outriggers and Poleholders. When fishing's your game, these are as important as the tackle you prize so highly and probably every bit as expensive to replace. Most outriggers are sturdy affairs of brass and bronze, chrome-plated, so there's not much chance of corrosion. Take a look at the fastenings though—these should be through-bolted to the deck or coaming and kept tight. Check the screws and locks on the tilt for any broken hardware. A touch of graphite on the moving parts will keep them working smoothly.

Fighting Chairs. If your cruiser doubles as a fishing machine, add these to your upkeep list. Most chairs are of aluminum but the anodizing can wear off and corrosion set in. Sand this off, prime the spots and use a clear epoxy cover. Lubricate the tilt and swivel hardware, and check the Dacron covers. The stitching and snaps can go on these.

MAINTENANCE AT THE HELM STATION

Whether your helm is on a flying bridge or in the deckhouse, most of your running time is spent there, so make sure everything works smoothly with no little nagging worries to bug you. Here's what should get your attention:

Steering System. Begin your check by swinging the wheel over hard to feel for any play in the cables or linkage, signalling trouble with the gear below. If there is, jot down a reminder to get at it when you do the below-deck maintenance, covered in the next section.

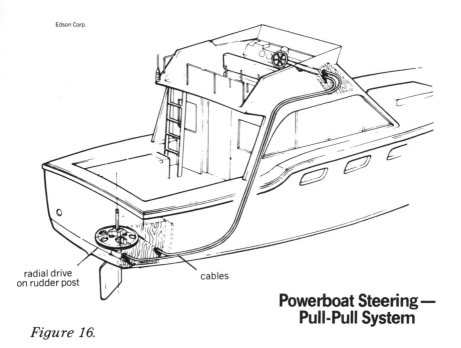

radial drive
on rudder post

cables

**Powerboat Steering —
Pull-Pull System**

Figure 16.

Hydraulic Booster. Where this is part of the steering system, maintenance is a bit different than with a Teleflex or the older wire-cable and sheaves arrangement. A regular hydraulic system is a fairly complex collection of pumps, cylinders, high-pressure lines, valves, etc. that really requires professional servicing. Have a qualified mechanic at the yard do it or an outside specialist. You can do a few checks yourself like looking for leaks. We'll take this up in the next section.

The Engine Controls. These should work smoothly when you move the throttle and clutch levers in the control case. Salt spray can work inside, so keep the parts clean and lubricate them at least several times during the season. Any hesitation or slack in the flexible cables to the engine can mean trouble so go over them when you do the jobs below deck.

The Compass. No question it's the most important instrument at the helm station, and the one you have to be dependent on most for accuracy. Has it been compensated in the last year? Most boatmen call this "swinging the compass" and if you've made any changes in equipment around the compass, adding electric motors for example, it may have been thrown off. It's not hard to compensate a compass, but you can have a pro do it and at the same time let him check for any internal bugs that might have also developed.

Engine Instruments. The array of these on some of the newer boats rivals a 747 panel, but the basics (temperature, rpms, oil pressure and ammeter) are the important ones to monitor when you're running. If any faults developed during the season, your annual maintenance is the time to have them repaired. And remember to check the panel lights, too —they may burn out unnoticed.

The Electronics. Here's where following a few basic rules of maintenance will save expensive servicing fees. Wherever possible, install instruments like a depth sounder, radio, RDF, etc. so they can be disconnected and stowed below. When this isn't practical, make sure they have Dacron covers to protect the inside plastic from moisture and from the sun's heat.

The corrosion of metal parts from salt spray is the bugaboo of all onboard electronics. To help prevent it, use one of the anti-corrosive sprays like WD-40 on all exposed metal parts. With the plethora of electronics on many boats today, the wiring connecting them is often a mare's nest where it wends its way below. To neaten it up, bundle related wires together for fast identification. If you don't have a diagram of the electronic system onboard, it will pay you to make one or have a service technician do it.

Upkeep of Other Gear. While you're working at the helm station, give some thought to whatever else may need attention. Feel the wiper blades for example. Has the rubber hardened so that it could scratch the windshield? Are the motors working okay?—salt spray can raise hob with their innards. How about the hardware that swings up the windshields?

Any corrosion that needs cleaning? And some oil on the moving parts will help too.

Topside Upkeep of Power- and Sailboats

Though their superstructures may vary a bit, maintenance of deckhouses and cabins remains the same for both types of boats. They also share a lot of similar gear above decks—lifelines, rails, ventilators, anchor windlasses, etc. Following are the areas and equipment that usually need inspection and upkeep:

DECKHOUSES AND CABINS

These are a good starting point because you can make the needed repairs and avoid running paint drippings down after you've done the decks and other gear below. The masthead washdown we suggested earlier should leave the tops of houses and cabin trunks in clean condition so you can do any spruceup work. Treatment for house sides is the same as that for fiberglass, wood, and metal, covered in the previous section.

On painting and varnishing deckhouses, cabins and their trim, see "Paints and Painting" at the end of the previous section. The Paint Chart there will help in selecting finishes for these areas. For places where a sure footing is needed, follow the method already outlined to get a nonskid finish.

PORTS AND WINDOWS

These are likely spots for leaks to develop during the season, and when you're working above deck is the time to fix them. Use a hose to help spot those around port frames and in channels of sliding windows where drains get plugged. The sealing around companionways and fittings on cabin trunks are other sources of leaks. Use a good sealant to fix them, then test with the hose again. If there are seams where the house sides and deck are joined, check carefully for leaks.

HATCHES, COMPANIONWAYS AND VENTILATORS

When you've finished with the superstructure, turn your attention to any needed upkeep on these. Depending on the material of the hatch covers, give them the repairs and cosmetic work outlined in the previous section. Check the hardware on hatches for any signs of corrosion, loose fastenings or broken parts. Where there's a rubber gasket or seal on the cover, make sure it's soft and keeping out water. Inspect the seam at the deck around the bases of hatches, this can crack and cause leaks below.

Ventilators should also get your attention, especially the Dorade type on sailboats which can leak. On ventilators with an exhaust fan built in, the motors are usually permanently lubricated but older types may need oiling. All screens in ventilators should be cleaned and the broken ones replaced.

The companionway may also need some upkeep. Wooden slides can warp causing the top to jam and doors to remain ajar. If there are any problems with this, a little fine-tuning work on the slides and top with a plane or chisel should remedy it. A wax lubricant will ease the way. The hardware too may need work if anyone has tried to spring the lock and hasp. And look at the screening to make sure there are no holes for the little devils to get in and bug you on a hot night.

LIFELINES, RAILS, STANCHIONS, LADDERS, PULPITS

These take the brunt of weather and sea, especially at the joints and deck plates, where galvanic corrosion can take place. Test all the stanchions for loose fastenings. As we mentioned before, any slack in the lifelines can be taken up by tightening the turnbuckles. On worn coverings, follow the earlier suggestion for using small diameter plastic tubing to replace them. The pulpit on both power and sailboats should be rugged enough to take a man's weight while handling sail or heavy ground tackle. Make sure there are no cracks in the welds or deck plates.

THE HARDWARE ON DECK

We've already covered the deck fittings on sailboats but there's a variety of other hardware on both sail- and power-boats that often needs upkeep. This includes cleats for dock and mooring lines, plates for gas and water fills, anchor chocks, awning sockets, etc. All of these are subject to corrosion and the fastenings may loosen up. Make sure the water and fuel plates have holding chains for the caps.

The shoreside power outlet is another piece of deck hardware that should be checked. If you've had any trouble with the power supply during the season, check the plugs and connections. The cable may have breaks in the insulation. These can be fixed temporarily with electrician's tape, but too many breaks call for a new cable.

BUOYS AND LIFE RAFTS

On many boats, ring and horseshoe buoys are mounted in the rigging or on stanchions for emergency use. Where these are used, the buoys should be checked for broken coverings and worn cordage. The hardware and straps of the holders may also need replacing.

Life rafts are another piece of deck gear that should be given attention. The weather can deteriorate the netting and hardware, weakening it so it may fail in an emergency. Self-inflating rafts should be tested each season and the charges in the CO_2 cylinders checked. Survival kits for rafts on deep-water boats should be inspected to make sure the contents haven't been affected by moisture and salt-water corrosion.

WINDLASSES, CAPSTANS AND BOW ROLLERS

The windlasses can range from a simple, manual type on a small sailboat where not much can get out of whack, up to an automatic anchoring system with fancy electronics on bigger cruisers. The typical electric windlass runs on battery power, and any maintenance should begin by following instructions in the service manual.

Bow rollers are like having an extra hand aboard because they can take so much strain out of getting up the hook. About the only maintenance the roller needs is occasional lubrication of the bearings.

Keeping Up the Decks

This is usually a priority job in any above-deck maintenance not only because the decks take a beating from sea and weather but also from the wear and tear of crew activities. Deck leaks are a nuisance to living below and, even more seriously, pose the threat of dry rot in a wooden hull. Leaks can also damage the backup blocks on deck fittings in a fiberglass hull and cause rust in a metal one. Since the repair of decks varies for different materials, we'll take them up in turn.

FIBERGLASS DECKS

These are usually a one-piece moulding in most hulls, joined at the gunwales. The seams are generally behind a rub strake and, unless the boat is seriously damaged, they rarely leak. Most glass decks have a moulded-in non-slip pattern which can trap tar and get badly stained. Use a mild solvent and stiff brush to remove. Where the surface isn't moulded, but is badly weathered and worn smooth, the only way to keep it up may be to prime and paint the fiberglass. Check the Paint Chart at the end of the previous section for recommended finishes, including a nonskid one.

When a wooden or metal deck is covered with fiberglass, the covering may peel away at the edges where the bond is weak. This calls for replacement of the damaged area and unless you have the expertise in working with resin and cloth, let a pro do the job. If the surface is only weathered, give it the same treatment with primer and paint as you would a regular glass deck.

WOODEN DECKS

Though a laid or planked deck is one of the hardest to maintain, if it's bright-finished it can be a handsome accent to a boat's appearance. On teak decks, a cleaning and light sanding will remove surface dirt and one of the teak "restorers," followed by a sealer, will help to preserve it. Painted decks are about the easiest to maintain—often a light sanding and fresh paint is all that's needed.

Where a deck plank is badly damaged from either dry rot or an accident, replacement is best handled by a professional. The bright-finished deck we mentioned earlier looks great but needs work to keep up. In some cases, this may call for complete refinishing down to the bare wood, followed by several coats of a urethane varnish. You'll have a thing of beauty, but it can also be as slippery as a skating rink in wet weather—so admire them on someone else's boat, not yours.

METAL DECKS

On many aluminum and steel hulls the decks are often covered with fiberglass, whose maintenance we outlined before. Where this isn't used, you can keep the metal in good condition by following the upkeep steps for metal hulls that we covered in the previous section.

RECAULKING DECK SEAMS

On a planked deck, these can be a source of leaks when the compound has cracked, dried or pulled out of the seams. Begin the recaulking by scraping out the old material, using a triangular tool or one made from the tang of a file that's been heated, bent and then ground to a shape that just fits in the seam. Make sure you get all the old compound out, then clean the space with a solvent.

Use a caulking gun with a cartridge of synthetic-rubber compound, filling the seam slightly higher than the surface

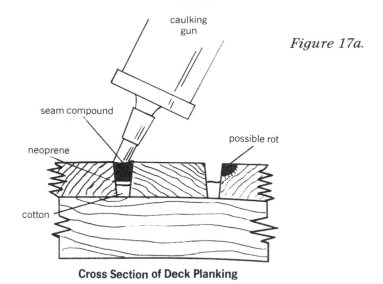

Figure 17a.

Cross Section of Deck Planking

Figure 17b. Filling deck seams with synthetic rubber compound. Masking tape keeps surplus off deck and makes cleanup job easier.

around it, then pressing it down with a putty knife. It will shrink slightly when it cures. Laying down masking tape on either side of the seam will keep it from getting on the planking. Let the compound cure until it's tacky but not too hard. If it's too soft, you'll pull it back out of the seam—too hard, it will tear along the edges.

THE CANVAS ABOVE DECK

By this we don't mean sails which have no interest for a powerboat man. What we are talking about are the many uses for canvas and Dacron on both power- and sailboats—things like cockpit and canopy covers, wind screens, wheel and instrument covers, etc. In addition, the rag man will think of his sailcovers (those on winches etc.), while the power man remembers Bimini tops, fly-bridge covers or the sun screens on deckhouse windows. The table below lists marine fabrics, their pros and cons and typical uses.

In any case, an inventory of the canvas above deck on the average boat will surprise the owner. And since it's there to offer protection, it makes good sense to keep it up. Your topside canvas should be part of the overall washdown we talked about earlier. A stiff bristle brush and judicious use of a plastic pot scrubber will loosen most of the caked-on dirt and seagull mess from the fabric. Stubborn stains may need the use of one of the chemical cleaners that marine-supply stores sell. In spite of the mildew treatment given most marine fabrics, some spores will attach themselves and build up a growth in time. Most of it will come off with a cleaner like "Mold-Away" or something similar. A mild solution of household bleach will also do the trick but try it out on a small area first to make sure it won't take out the color. Always hose off all cleaners with fresh water.

While you're cleaning the fabric, take a look at the frames and hardware that support it and the fasteners holding the cover in place. Where there's corrosion of the metal, sand it off, prime and paint with epoxy. The teeth on marine zippers are tough but will break off and jam the slide—also look for broken stitching on the closures. A sailmaker or canvas man

TYPES OF MARINE FABRICS

FABRIC	ADVANTAGES	DISADVANTAGES	TYPICAL USES
Canvas (Untreated)	Relatively low cost. "Breathability" permits free air circulation, helps stop condensation. Easy to fabricate. Seams seal tight when wet. Strength increases 25% when wet. Available in many colors.	Will mildew or rot unless treated. Increases in weight and stiffness when wet, is then harder to handle. Long drying time before storage. Stretches and shrinks unless treated. Stains easily, retains dirt. Shorter service life.	Winter storage covers. Awnings. Deck gear covers. Cockpit covers and curtains.
Vinyl-coated Canvas	Relatively low cost. Good resistance to weathering. Smooth surface—no weave to trap dirt. Easy to fabricate, heat sealable.	Eliminates many disadvantages of regular canvas but still heavy weight and stiff. Not suitable for winter covers. Doesn't "breathe."	Cockpit covers. Dodgers and wind screens. Ventilation a "must" under covers.
Dacron Polyester	Built-in resistance to mildew and rot. Lighter than canvas —easier to handle, also stronger. Won't shrink or stretch. Good weatherability. Easy to clean. Translucent, admits light.	Higher cost than canvas. Harder to fabricate. Doesn't "breathe"; needs vents for air circulation. Seams can leak. Fabric requires waterproofing.	Cockpit covers and curtains. Fly bridge tops. Windshield covers. Air scoops. Deck gear covers. Bimini tops.
Vinyl-coated Dacron Polyester	Combines outstanding weathering qualities of vinyl with stabilizing qualities of Dacron. Permanent outdoor colors. Flame retardent. Easy to fabricate. Heat sealable. Resists dirt, bird droppings.	Fabric doesn't admit air, needs vents in covers to stop condensation. Higher cost than canvas.	Boat tops. Cockpit curtains. Wind screen. Fly bridge covers.

Figure 18. Bimini top of light, translucent Dacron is typical above-deck canvas on a powerboat. Same fabric is used for flybridge cover shown below it.

can repair them both and do it on the boat since many have sewing machines inside their vans. They can also replace all kinds of fasteners and grommets in the fabric. You can replace the parts that are on the boat—marine-supply stores sell them with self-tapping screws attached.

During the season, always repair tears and holes immediately—don't let the rip spread. You can get small patches and cement from most canvas shops and in a pinch, even use adhesive tape as a temporary repair. Where you find metal or part of the boat's structure chafing the fabric, insulate the spot with tape or sew a reinforcement in the canvas to prevent it.

In time, even the best maintained canvas and Dacron will need replacing. If the cover is small, bring it to the shop to use as a pattern for a new one. Where it's too big, have the canvas man come out and do the measuring—don't do it yourself or you'll be responsible for the fit. Incidentally, while most marine fabrics today are preshrunk, there's always some slight "setting" on a custom-tailored cover after it's been up for a few weeks. The maker builds in an allowance for this so don't blast him for a poor fit. Have a little patience and it will probably work out.

Last, but certainly not least, always be sure there's enough ventilation under a cover. This is doubly important for Dacron and vinyl-covered fabrics which don't "breathe" like canvas. The ventilation should be built into the cover. There are several devices on the market like "Posi-Vents" that admit air without letting in water. Snap-fastened covers usually get some ventilation between the closures but tightly zippered ones don't and need other means.

TAKING CARE OF THE DINK

If you use one of these faithful friends, whether it's a fancy yacht tender, a glass dinghy or the popular inflatable, give it some tender loving care. Start with a thorough cleaning and hosing. For any needed repairs, see the suggestions for different materials in the previous section on hull work. The Paint Chart at the end of that section will help on this score.

Inflatables require very little maintenance when they're

properly used. These "instant boats" are virtually indestruct-ible—they'll bounce off almost anything you hit. If punctures do occur, repairs are easily made with the kit and instruc-tions that come with the boat. Replacement kits can be bought at marine-supply stores.

Fixing a puncture is like putting a patch on an air mat-tress, if you've ever done camping. While it's better to let the repair cure overnight, you can in an emergency inflate the damaged chamber after an hour but at a reduced pressure. If you have trouble finding a leak, inflate the boat to a higher pressure and listen for a hissing sound. Another way is to sponge on a 10% solution of dish detergent and watch for the telltale bubbles that will pinpoint the leak. When you're using an inflatable, try to keep the inside bottom of the boat dry. Water can accumulate there and corrode the hardware that holds the plywood floor in place, eventually damaging the wood itself.

3. The Maintenance Below

In the first section of this book, we described the work on the hull as being the most important part of any maintenance program, and that is still true. But keeping up the area below decks is a close runner-up for some obvious reasons. In some ways, this space on a cruising boat is like the interior of a space craft in that both telescope all the living functions of those aboard into a relatively small space along with supporting equipment. All this makes the job of maintaining below decks more difficult than the areas we covered before.

In addition to keeping everything below in good operating condition, it must also be protected from corrosion, safeguarded against fire and explosion, and supplied with fresh air to prevent condensation and dry rot.

This may sound like a tall order for any maintenance program but by tackling the jobs in logical order and in small doses, you can handle most of them yourself. Make a list promptly of those jobs that require more expertise than you can muster, so you can get an early slot in the work schedule of the marina or yard.

The Engine Compartment

Begin your upkeep work below here even though "compartment" may only dignify the space around a small diesel tucked under the cockpit floor of a sailboat. Before you roll up your sleeves though, check the engine-hour meter and log book to see how long since the last work was done on the power plant. If all that's needed is a tuneup, make a date with the yard for it or with an outside mechanic. 250 hours is usually considered average between tuneups—500 hours for a major overhaul on gas engines. In doing any engine work yourself, it's a good idea to follow the manufacturer's service manual.

To simplify the work in the engine compartment, we've divided the normal maintenance there into these sections:

1. Gasoline Engines
2. Diesel Engines
3. Sterndrive Equipment Inside the Hull (The outside parts were covered in Section 1, "The Hull Work.")

Note: Some of the jobs listed below are for putting the engines back in commission after layup for storage which is covered again in the last section of the book.

Gasoline Engines

Here's what is generally done to keep them running at peak efficiency during the season:

SEA-WATER COOLING SYSTEMS

Where this has been winterized, open the plugs at the bottom of the blocks and manifolds to drain out the antifreeze. Refill the system with fresh water, turn over the engine and check for leaks. Make sure the belts on the water pumps are

tight and in good condition. The pumps should also be lubricated with a special grease for this purpose. If you haven't
replaced the thermostats in the system, do it now. These
should be changed at least once a year—make sure you get
the same operating temperature on the new ones.

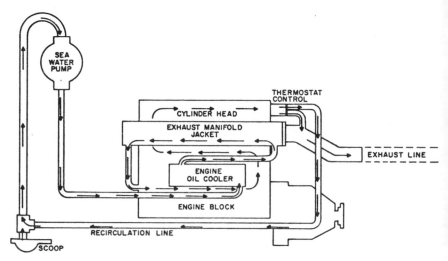

*Figure 19. Sea-water cooling system of gasoline engine.
Thermostat controls temperature of recirculated water in
block which then flows out the exhaust line.*

FRESH-WATER COOLING SYSTEMS

If this has been winterized, give it the same treatment as
for the sea-water system above. Check the belts on both the
fresh- and sea-water pumps and look for any leaks in hoses
or fittings. The reserve tank on a fresh-water cooling system
should be kept filled at all times. In some systems, a mixture
of 50% water 50% antifreeze is used as the coolant.

HEAT EXCHANGERS

These are an important part of a freshwater cooling system and need periodic servicing. Sea water, circulating around a core of tubes, cools the fresh water inside which in turn actually cools the engine—hence the use of the word "exchanger." While inlet strainers will stop most of the foreign matter in the sea water, salt deposits can build up in the shell and rust from the engine block can collect in the tubes of the core (the core is usually removable for servicing). In time, both kinds of deposits must be removed which means pulling the exchanger out of the boat and sending it to a shop specializing in this work.

In addition to a heat exchanger in the cooling-water system, some diesel engines also have them in the lube oil and transmission fluid coolers. These are usually smaller than

Figure 20.

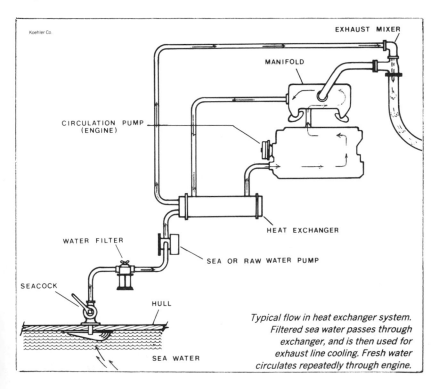

Koehler Co.

EXHAUST MIXER

MANIFOLD

CIRCULATION PUMP
(ENGINE)

HEAT EXCHANGER

WATER FILTER

SEA OR RAW WATER PUMP

SEACOCK

HULL

SEA WATER

*Typical flow in heat exchanger system.
Filtered sea water passes through
exchanger, and is then used for
exhaust line cooling. Fresh water
circulates repeatedly through engine.*

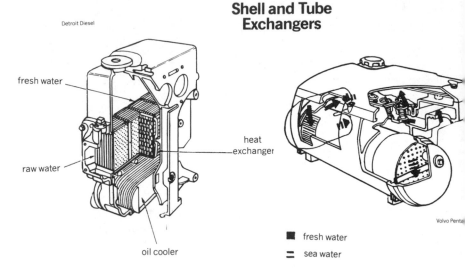

Shell and Tube Exchangers

Detroit Diesel

fresh water

raw water

heat exchanger

oil cooler

Volvo Penta

■ fresh water

☰ sea water

Figure 21. Cell and housing design exchanger (left) circulates sea water horizontally—engine coolant flows from top to bottom. This combination coolant/oil cooler can be used with smaller engine-gear combinations. Engine coolant exchanger (right) returns coolant directly to engine until thermostats open (as shown). Then both salt and fresh water travel separately from one end of cooler to the other and back.

the main exchanger but still require periodic cleaning. The manufacturer's service manual will give you the details on this operation.

FUEL-SUPPLY SYSTEM

Where a gasoline engine has been winterized, pull off the tape seal around the screen on the flame arrestor and, if it hasn't been done before, clean off any carbon on it with kerosene.

If the engine hasn't been laid up, begin the upkeep of the fuel system by checking all lines and fittings, shutoff valves, etc. for leaks. The filters in the fuel line should be cleaned and those with removable elements replaced. Most engines usually have a small, in-line filter on the feed going into the carburetor which requires replacing the ceramic cartridge inside.

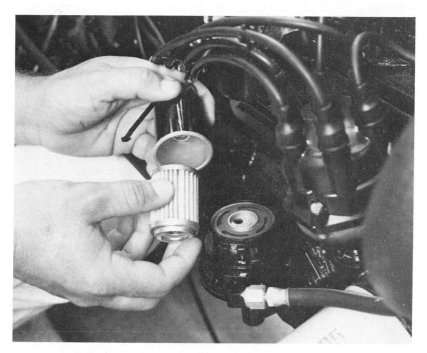

Figure 22. Checking gasoline fuel filter (mounted on top of fuel pump). Cartridge should be replaced every 50 hours of running time.

LUBRICATION SYSTEM

In a marine engine, this is the same as the lube system in your car, requiring an oil change whenever the service manual calls for it. You should also replace the filter at the same time. But unlike car engines, changing the oil in a boat usually involves a hand pump to drain out the old oil because the drain plug is often down in the bilge and inaccessible. Before you do the change, warm up the engine so that any deposits will be dissolved and drained out at the same time. Use the pump in the dipstick hole and let the oil run into a bucket. Refill the crankcase with new oil and check the level. Next, take off the oil filler cap, clean the filter inside with kerosene then reoil it and replace the cap on the engine.

Figure 23. Draining engine crankcase with a hand pump in dipstick tube. Oil filter should be replaced with each change, about every 100 hours of engine time or whenever service manual recommends.

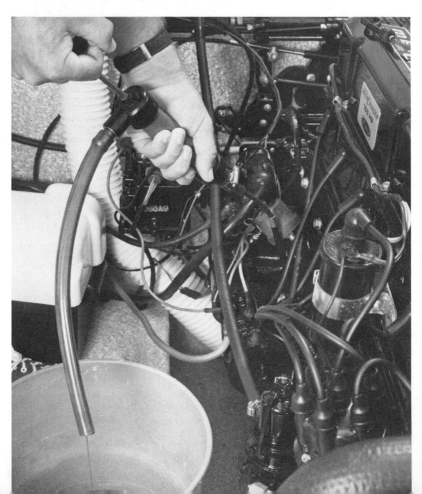

ENGINE ELECTRICAL SYSTEM

Here again, the components are similar to those in your car, but on a boat they're more affected by vibrations from the engine running at a constant speed over long periods, and by dampness and corrosion from salt air.

Wiring. This is particularly prone to dampness and the extremes of temperature in a crowded engine compartment. Give all the wiring a check for cracks, and replace any needed parts with a marine type. Break apart the connecting plugs and remove any green crust that may have collected on the contacts.

Alternator. The output of this should be monitored regularly during the season by checking the ammeter on the instrument panel. Any signs of a drop in alternator output calls for a thorough checkout by a specialist. The adjustment on it is too delicate for any do-it-yourself tinkering. If a diode has burned out, the unit may need to be replaced. Most alternators have sealed bearings making lubrication unnecessary, but you should check the belt tension to make sure it isn't slipping.

Ignition Care. This is the heart of the electrical system since the distributor and coil produce the spark distributed to the plugs. Start by checking the harness wiring for cracks where moisture can penetrate and short-circuit the current. Too many cracks should mean replacing the whole business. Next, take the distributor cap off and check for cracks in the plastic. Inspect the breaker points inside and if they have a deposit, clean it off with an ignition file (like a small nail file). If they're badly pitted, get a replacement kit containing new points. The kit usually has instructions on adjusting the breaker-point gap between them to meet the specifications in your engine service manual. Before you replace the rotor, clean the contacts on the arm, then put a few drops of oil on the shaft before you snap the distributor cap back on.

Incidentally, if you have any trouble with damp wiring,

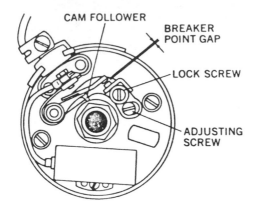

CAM FOLLOWER
BREAKER POINT GAP
LOCK SCREW
ADJUSTING SCREW

Figure 24. Top view of distributor with cap removed showing position of breaker points. Gap should be adjusted to meet specification in engine service manual.

Figure 25. Measuring gap in spark plug with a feeler gauge. Space between electrodes should check with engine service manual when plugs are cleaned or replaced.

causing hard engine-starting during the season, keep a can of chemical spray that will dry it out quickly on hand.

While the starter motor isn't really part of the electrical system, it should be checked if there were any problems during the season. Give the cable to it from the battery a look-see for breaks or worn insulation. The solenoids in the relay switch that controls the starter should snap over promptly when you hit the button—any lag can mean a hard starting problem next season.

TRANSMISSION UPKEEP

Add this to your list of regular chores when the boat is in commission, checking the hydraulic-fluid level and adding any if needed. Also take a look at the color of the fluid which should be a reddish brown; but if water has leaked into the transmission case, it turns a cloudy coffee-color. In that case, call in a specialist to find the cause and correct it. Follow your service manual for the proper time to change the fluid —usually about every 100 hours of running time. This is another tricky area because the drain plug is at the bottom of the transmission, so use a hand pump.

CHECKING BELTS

These make the forward end of most marine engines look like a factory with at least two, and sometimes more, belts driving the alternator, water and hydraulic pumps, etc. The tension on them is important and should be tested regularly when you're doing other service chores. Press the belt down in the middle of its driving distance. It should go down about a half inch if the tension is right. Too loose and the belt will slip—too tight and it will wear out quickly. Where there's any evidence of wear and fraying, replace it from the spares most owners carry aboard.

ENGINE-COMPARTMENT VENTILATION

The risk of a potential explosion from gas vapors in the

bilge has been stressed so much in boating magazines and books that it may seem redundant to bring it up again here. However, when you're working below, there's no better time to ask yourself if the bilge ventilation in your boat is adequate. The Coast Guard feels it's so important they have strict rules for the ventilation of engine compartments. Among other things, the rules specify minimum ratings for blower capacity, duct size and location, etc. If you have any doubts about your own exhaust blower system, the time to boost it is when you're doing engine work. Installing bigger blowers or adding another one is not that difficult. It's also a good idea to make sure the plastic duct hoses go deep enough into the bilge to pick up gas fumes.

On the maintenance of blowers, most of the motors have sealed bearings that don't require lubrication. You should

Figure 26. Powered ventilation system in engine compartment exhausts fumes and gasoline vapors trapped in bilges, reducing risk of accidental explosion.

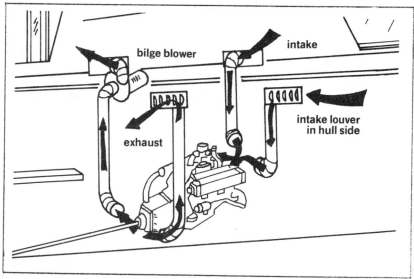

check the wiring to them, though, for any breaks that could cause an accidental explosion.

Diesel Engines

Since they have fewer parts than a gasoline engine and will run longer between major overhauls, diesels require less upkeep during the season. However, they still need some servicing on a regular basis and a complete checkout of certain critical parts at annual maintenance time—not only to ensure their smooth operation but also to protect the sizeable investment most owners have in the engines.

Figure 27. Parts of a typical marine diesel engine. Not visible are the filters which remove water and impurities from the fuel supply.

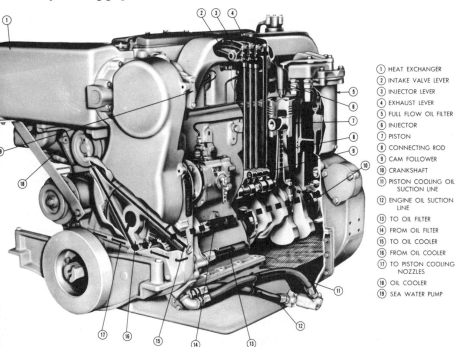

1. HEAT EXCHANGER
2. INTAKE VALVE LEVER
3. INJECTOR LEVER
4. EXHAUST LEVER
5. FULL FLOW OIL FILTER
6. INJECTOR
7. PISTON
8. CONNECTING ROD
9. CAM FOLLOWER
10. CRANKSHAFT
11. PISTON COOLING OIL SUCTION LINE
12. ENGINE OIL SUCTION LINE
13. TO OIL FILTER
14. FROM OIL FILTER
15. TO OIL COOLER
16. FROM OIL COOLER
17. TO PISTON COOLING NOZZLES
18. OIL COOLER
19. SEA WATER PUMP

While service manuals vary, here is a brief rundown on the key points to keep in mind when you're working in the engine compartment. For the specifics, use your own service manual as a bible.

COOLING SYSTEM

Most diesels use a fresh-water cooling system, so follow the care we outlined earlier for gasoline engines. The parts to check here are the hoses, pumps and heat exchanger which requires servicing as we described before. If you find deposits building up regularly in the shell and core of the exchanger, it may pay you to install a water-conditioning unit in the system to remove silt and rust before it goes into the exchanger.

FUEL-SUPPLY SYSTEM

The upkeep of this is more critical on a diesel because there are more filters in the supply line and the engine depends on a supply of clean, water-free oil for smooth operation. The fuel tanks should be cleaned at least once during the season (more often if you have any suspicions about some dockside fuel) to avoid water contamination and remove the sediment stirred up by the boat rolling. Primary and secondary fuel filters and water separators should be serviced regularly, draining the water and sediment and replacing the elements if necessary. When you do this, it's a good idea to put in new gaskets on the filter units. The fuel transfer pump should also be cleaned periodically of any sediment—the service manual should help on this.

The injectors in the cylinders are other parts that require regular cleaning and calibrating as does the injection pump itself. While most engine service manuals have instructions for doing these jobs, if you don't have the expertise have a qualified mechanic do it.

AIR FILTERS

Diesel engines require a lot more air to operate than a

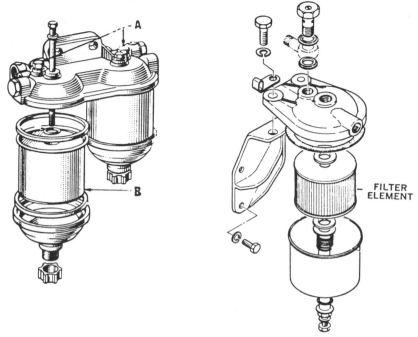

*Figure 28. Fuel filters on diesel engine: Dual-type filter (left),
A) bleed screws, B) replaceable element. Exploded view of
secondary filter (right). Fuel enters and exits from the top
cover.*

*Figure 29. Changing diesel fuel filter which removes water.
Replacement is about every 250 hours of engine running
time.*

gasoline engine, so check the air filters regularly. Blow out any dirt in them and if there's too much build-up, replace the elements.

LUBRICATION SYSTEM

The maintenance of this is similar to the lube system in a gasoline engine. Change the crankcase oil and filter and again follow the service manual for the time interval and recommended grade of oil. You may have to use the hand-pump routine we outlined earlier. Before you take out the old oil, make sure the engine is hot so you can drain out any sludge and dirt as well. Problems with oil pressure falling off when the engine is operating can mean trouble with the pump, so have it checked and fixed.

TRANSMISSION CARE

On a diesel, this is similar to the upkeep on a gasoline engine; it includes checking the fluid level regularly and, at the same time, looking at the color for any signs of water leakage into the housing. The hydraulic fluid should be changed according to the service manual, using a hand pump for the job.

EXHAUST SYSTEM

While there isn't the danger of carbon monoxide from diesel exhaust, the pipes and mufflers can rust and corrode especially at connections. When they do, the smell can be traced back to the trouble spots which should be fixed before the boat goes back in the water.

Though the Coast Guard rules we mentioned earlier apply only to gasoline-powered boats, ventilating a diesel engine is almost as important. For one thing, it requires a lot more air in operation so most builders put in good-sized vents with cowls to scoop in air. In some cases they also install a blower system which can be a blessing to those aboard who suffer from seasickness. There's nothing like hot diesel fumes to make you feel queasy on a day with little wind.

SPRUCEUP THE ENGINE

When you're all finished with the engine maintenance, clean off the grease and dirt with one of the gunk-remover sprays or better still have the yard steam clean it. Use one of the heat-resistant engine paints, masking off the metal parts and wiring. This will make it a lot easier to spot leaks from oil lines and head gaskets, and to clean up any spills from service chores. On the exposed metal parts (except those that get hot), you can stop rust from forming by using one of the anti-corrosive sprays.

Inside Sterndrive Maintenance

With the upkeep on engines completed, let's move on to the care of another part of the power package that may be in the compartment, the inside sterndrive unit. We covered the outside maintenance of this earlier in the first section of the book. Inside or out, you should follow the manufacturer's service manual. Here are the upkeep jobs usually done on the inside sterndrive unit:

TRANSOM MOUNTING

Inspect this for any cracks in the housing or loose fastenings—tighten all those you can reach. Lubricate the grease fittings on the pivot points with a low-pressure hand gun. Their locations will vary from one drive to another but make sure you do them all.

THROTTLE AND SHIFT CONTROLS

There are different systems for these but all the components should be checked for any signs of loose fastenings, chafe and wear, especially at the contact and connection points. Is there any excess play in the controls when you work them? Try to locate and correct it—if you can't, have the dealer or a serviceman check it out. Some control linkages have grease fittings on moving parts—lubricate these with a hand gun. Your service manual usually has a chart of their locations.

HYDRAULIC SYSTEM

When your sterndrive has power trim and tilt (most have the last), go over the connections on the hydraulic lines inside and look for any leaks. Check the fluid level in the reservoir when you're in the engine compartment—some have a built-in dipstick for this. Where the level is low, add whatever brand the manufacturer recommends. A persistently low level may mean a leak somewhere in the system either in the lines or cylinders—look for droppings below them. If they show up, have a specialist locate the leaks and fix them. They may be in the connections so tighten these first and you may save a repair bill.

STEERING CONTROL

This varies with the sterndrive unit. If yours has a mechanical steering cable, it should be lubricated. Also grease the fitting where the cable comes out of the tube, but make sure it is retracted when you do this. If it isn't, the lubricant may keep the cable from going back in and you'll get a hydraulic lock, even though it's a mechanical system. On twin sterndrives, the linkage between the units usually requires some form of lubrication. Look for any excess play here, too.

BATTERIES—THEIR CARE AND FEEDING

Make these part of your regular maintenance checks while the boat is in service—checking the electrolyte level and the charge in each cell. Use distilled water (if available) and a rubber bulb to add fluid; a hydrometer to check the specific gravity and the charge. Try to get balanced readings in the cells—too wide a variation may mean a dead cell and replacing the battery. The new one should have equal ampere capacity and be a marine type.

The cables connecting the battery to the starter motor and engine block carry a heavy load of current. Any breaks in the insulation may cause a short circuit or other trouble, so give them a close inspection. Signs of damage call for replacement of the cable.

Your battery care during the season should also include keeping the terminals free of lead sulphate deposits which also build up on the cable lugs. Remove these from the terminals and sand- or wire-brush them clean. If any are too badly corroded, replace the lugs. Before connecting them, smear on a coating of Vaseline to stop the sulphate from building again. Any accidental spills of acid can be cleaned up with a bicarb solution.

The mounting for batteries on some boats is often in a hard-to-reach spot, of flimsy wooden construction and without a tray to catch acid spills. It's not only a mess but can be dangerous in a seaway should the batteries shift and work loose. If your mounting leaves something to be desired, have

Figure 30. Sterndrive maintenance. Lubricating steering cable with hand gun. High pressure gun should not be used.

a new one installed of heavy construction with a lead or plastic tray and chocks to keep the batteries in place. Try to locate it where it's easy to service the batteries and not near any hot parts of the engine or exhaust system.

ENGINE-CONTROL SYSTEMS

We've already touched on those that are part of a stern-drive but now we'd like to cover the systems generally used on regular inboard engine installations. The simplest of the clutch controls use a lever and rod linkage from the topsides station to the transmission on the engine. These are pretty rugged and only need occasional checking to make sure all the connections are tight. The contact points in the linkage should be lubricated at least once during the season.

Most of the throttle and clutch controls on boats today use a flexible cable system (like "Teleflex") to connect the helm station with the engine. The upkeep here is to make sure all the cable connections are tight and to lubricate all moving parts. If you find any excess play in the system, you can take it up by adjusting the cable at the terminals.

MANUAL STEERING SYSTEMS

Keeping up the topsides parts of these has been described in the previous section, but here's what's involved in maintaining the gear below decks and usually in the engine compartment.

On smaller boats, a rack-and-pinion system is often used to connect the steering wheel and the rudder. Check for play by spinning the wheel over hard and if you feel any, tighten up the turnbuckles in the cables. Make sure the parts connected to the wheel are lubricated so it isn't hard to turn. If there are any cables check them for signs of wear and see that all the fittings are tight, especially those at the rudder.

Another type of steering system uses a drum on the steering wheel and cables running through sheaves back to a quadrant on the rudder which turns it. The upkeep on this is to check the cable for signs of fraying and the corner blocks to make sure they are well lubricated and the mountings haven't cracked. Here again, any excess play in the wheel can be taken up by shortening the cables at the turnbuckles.

HYDRAULIC STEERING SYSTEMS

These work on a similar principle to the power steering in your car. When the boat's steering wheel is turned, the hydraulic pressure from an engine-driven pump actuates the rudder by means of cylinders connected to it. A hydraulic system is complex and, other than periodically checking the lines for leaks and making sure the reservoir is full of fluid, any needed repairs and adjustments should be done by a specialist. Booster systems should also be checked by him.

ENGINE MOUNTS

Before winding up your work in the engine compartment, take a look at the bolts holding the engine down to make sure they are tight; look also at those through the mounts into the hull. Some owners believe it's a good policy to have a mechanic check the engine alignment at some point during the annual maintenance. Fiberglass hulls have a tendency to work when they're in service and may actually bend slightly when hauled in a travel lift or derrick sling. This can cause the mounts to shift and throw off the alignment.

Other Below-Deck Work

With everything in the engine compartment given your eagle-eye scanning and put in good condition for the coming season, you can then turn your attention to the rest of the below-decks equipment. This is important too, for it helps keep your boat running and makes living there more comfortable and convenient.

FUEL TANKS AND LINES

Those in the engine space were covered before, but in some boats the tanks may be located elsewhere. Begin your upkeep of the fuel system at them, cleaning out the tanks at least once during the season to get rid of sediment and any water contamination. In diesels, this can clog the filters and damage the injection system. It can also raise Cain with the filters and carburetors on gasoline engines.

Start checking the lines at the shutoff valves to make sure the bronze in them hasn't seized up or there are any leaks. Follow the lines through to the engine, looking for brittleness at the unions in copper and spongy spots in Neoprene. Any evidence in either material should mean cutting out and replacing the bad sections. Check the repairs for leaks when the engines are running and there's pressure in the system.

Water-Supply Systems

Of all the equipment below decks, the water supply is most important to the health and well-being of those aboard to ensure a clean, adequate supply for drinking and cooking, plus showering. Whether it's simply a gravity-supply tank with a faucet at the end (as on many small boats) or a pressure system with automatic-demand pump and many outlets on larger craft, these are the checkpoints to keep in mind on the maintenance:

TANKS

These aren't that accessible tucked away in the bow or under the cabin sole, but you should flush them out at least once during the season. Here again, check the shutoff valve and connections to the filler and overflow pipes for leaks, even a small one can quickly rob you of water on a long cruise.

LINES

Most of those for cold water on boats today are of plastic tubing with cemented fittings so leaks along the line or at fittings are easily repaired. Hot-water lines are usually made of copper tubing which can crack from vibration. A section with a leak can be cut out and a new one installed using compression fittings. All water lines should be accessible for inspection. Some owners identify their purpose with tags from a hand-lettering machine. Make sure the lines are firmly anchored to stop chafing and vibration. If your boat is laid up for the winter in cold climates there should be some way of draining the lines or blowing them out to prevent freezing.

VALVES AND FITTINGS

These can be another source of leaks, so check all those in the system. In addition to the shutoff at the tank, a check or relief valve may be in the hot-water supply line, that keeps hot water from flowing back into the cold-water supply lines. They are also used in the line to a galley pump to keep it primed. You can get replacement discs and washers at most plumbing-supply stores.

Where there's a dockside water connection, it may include a pressure-reducing valve to keep pressure aboard at a safe level. Check this valve for any leaks or parts that stick. And remember faucets and fixtures in the system may also need some maintenance. A slow leak can drain your tank in a sneaky way, especially in a telephone-type shower head hidden behind a curtain. Most replacement parts can be obtained from a plumbing or marine-supply store.

Care of Pressure Systems

These include a variety of types and sizes but here's what is usually done to keep them in good working order. Please remember these are general rules; follow the specifics in the service manual that came with your system.

PUMPS

These are the heart of a pressure system and consist mainly of two types. One type of pump, the centrifugal, is usually mounted at the end of a motor frame with bearings that may need lubrication. Some of these pumps depend on the water flow in the system to cool them, and can't be run

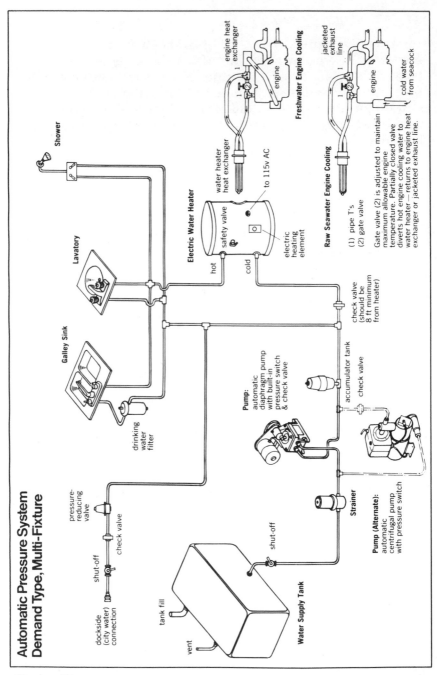

Automatic Pressure System
Demand Type, Multi-Fixture

Shower

Lavatory

Galley Sink

drinking water filter

pressure-reducing valve

check valve

shut-off

dockside (city water) connection

tank fill

vent

Water Supply Tank

shut-off

Strainer

Pump (Alternate):
automatic centrifugal pump with pressure switch

Pump:
automatic diaphragm pump with built-in pressure switch & check valve

accumulator tank

check valve

check valve (should be 8 ft minimum from heater)

hot

cold

Electric Water Heater

safety valve

water heater heat exchanger

to 115v AC

electric heating element

Freshwater Engine Cooling

engine heat exchanger

engine

1

Raw Seawater Engine Cooling

jacketed exhaust line

engine

1

cold water from seacock

(1) pipe T's
(2) gate valve

Gate valve (2) is adjusted to maintain maximum allowable engine temperature. Partially closed valve diverts hot engine cooling water to water heater—returns to engine heat exchanger or jacketed exhaust line.

Figure 31.

dry more than a few seconds without damaging the pump. The other kind of pump is the diaphragm, usually belt-driven by an electric motor with a built-in pressure switch and check valve, both of which should be checked.

Both kinds of pumps may have a "dry-tank" switch that automatically shuts off the motor, but requires resetting to start it. If you haven't a switch in the pump circuit, it's a good idea to install one for those times when no one is aboard. This keeps the pump from accidentally turning on and flooding the bilge. Make sure the wiring to all pump motors is in good condition and above the normal bilge-water level.

PRESSURE SWITCH

This is the sensor in an automatic-demand-type system that starts and stops the pump. If you have a leak somewhere, it can keep you awake nights, snapping on and off as the pressure drops and builds up again. The switches usually don't need much care but when they go bad you can get a replacement from the dealer or manufacturer.

ACCUMULATOR TANK

An accessory item in some systems for the purpose of storing up pressure so the pump doesn't have to run as often. The tank also eliminates "water hammer" (pounding in the pipes), and helps to deliver better flow to outlets farthest from the pump. There are no moving parts in an accumulator—just check the connections for leaks.

STRAINERS AND FILTERS

These are used between the supply tank and the pump to keep dirt and other particles from being circulated. Some strainers have a removable screen for cleaning. Filters usually have a replaceable element. Many systems also have a filter in the supply lines to drinking water outlets—often a point-of-use type under the sink. Some more sophisticated models are combination filters and purifiers that remove dirt and rust, along with bacteria and other organisms. Most have replaceable elements—just check the use-and-care booklet that comes with the unit.

HOT-WATER HEATERS

Once considered a luxury, these are now almost a necessity on cruising boats. The heaters come in various types, depending on the energy source. The simplest are faucet-water heaters that plug into the nearest 110-volt AC outlet. Not much to go on the fritz here but when they do, the answer is to replace the whole unit. Their disadvantage is that they are limited to heating water for one outlet only.

Propane bulkhead heaters are used a lot in Europe but only a small number are used in this country. They're a self-contained type that is installed at the outlet, and they do a good job. Their disadvantages are limited heating capacity and the fact the propane tank can be a hazard. If you use this type, follow the usual safety precautions for this kind of fuel.

ELECTRIC-TANK HEATERS

Like their shoreside domestic cousins, these heaters use an electric immersion element operating on 110-volt AC shoreside power to heat the water. The maintenance is pretty minimal, involving only the checking of plumbing connections for leaks, the thermostat that controls the temperature (usually adjustable) and the safety or relief valve. If trouble develops in any of these, you can get replacements from the manufacturer.

OFF-THE-ENGINE HEATERS

An economical way to heat water is to use the heat from the engine when it's running. One type operates by diverting some of the hot water from a jacketed exhaust, and using it to heat the water in a storage tank. This can either supplement an electric heater or it can use engine heat alone. Another type uses the hot water from the heat exchanger in a fresh-water, engine-cooling system to heat the water in a storage tank.

The maintenance of both types of heaters involves looking for leaks in the plumbing and checking the gate valve that diverts the hot water from the engine.

AUXILIARY GENERATOR SETS

These sets of below-deck equipment should also be on your maintenance schedule. Since the sets are a miniature version of the main engine, gasoline or diesel, they need the same periodic servicing, though on a much smaller scale. For this reason, you can follow the upkeep outlined earlier in this section under "The Engine Compartment." Please use this as a general guide but by all means follow the service manual from the manufacturer.

Air Conditioning and Heating Systems

The use of this equipment is part of a growing trend by boat owners to enjoy more of the amenities of shoreside living when they're cruising. But along with creature comforts, goes the chore of keeping these systems in good condition. Following are the points to keep in mind:

AIR CONDITIONERS

These run the gamut from small, self-contained units in a cabin-top or deckhouse to large, central systems for all the living areas on big boats. For upkeep of the self-contained models, use the service manual from the manufacturer. Unlike the typical window units in homes, some marine air conditioners transfer their heat to the sea water, using a pump to cool the condenser either in the unit itself or on larger models in a remote installation in the bilge. You can do most of the upkeep on the cooling-water system of the conditioner yourself, checking the intake screen and cleaning it, or replacing the element if there's a filter in the line. Look for any leaks in the plumbing and see if the pump motor needs lubricating—some have sealed bearings. Most air conditioners have removable filters at the air intake which should be cleaned (carefully, as they're fragile) or replaced. For service or repairs on any of the parts inside the unit—compressor, evaporator, temperature control, etc.—call in a pro to do the work.

Important: If you're installing an air conditioner for the first time be certain that the 110-volt AC line in the cabin or deckhouse will carry the load—some of the self-contained units pull up to 18 amperes.

Central Air Conditioning Systems. These are so complex that any service and upkeep work on them should be done by a specialist. It's no place for the do-it-yourself advocate as some of the jobs can be dangerous—recharging the Freon is one, so don't try it unless you have the experience and know how it should be done.

Reverse-Cycle Heating and Cooling. The first type of these units uses a special valve and supporting equipment to reverse the cooling cycle and provide heat. The other kind of unit is a combination refrigeration/cooling, electric-heating model. Both types are fairly complex and any service or repairs should be handled by a professional.

HEATERS

There are a variety of heat sources that can be used on a boat from portable electric heaters through stoves, fireplaces and hot-air systems that use oil or LP gas as fuels. The electric heaters require little maintenance—those mounted on a bulkhead have fan motors usually permanently lubricated. Some boats use oil-burning, hot-air heaters imported from Canada or Europe like the Webasto or Espar heaters. These are self-contained units that burn oil in a sealed combustion chamber vented to the outside air. Their operation is thermostatically controlled with an electric fan inside that circulates the hot air through ducts. Most operate on a 12- to 32-volt DC line and require no maintenance. If you're using a butane or propane gas heater like the bulkhead-mounted type, be sure the installation follows the manufacturer's recommendations for safe operation.

SHAFT LOG AND STUFFING BOXES

Since these penetrate the hull and can be a source of leaks, they should be part of your preventive maintenance below decks. The wear and damage to a sterntube and stuffing box can come from several causes. The most common is a change in the alignment between engine and shaft from vibration or a shift in the mounts, as we pointed out earlier. Another cause comes from running aground—an occurrence that can damage the propeller and transmit the shock to the log and stuffing box. A loose key or worn spline in the wheel and shaft can also set up vibration and result in damage.

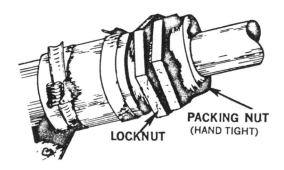

PACKING NUT
(HAND TIGHT)
LOCKNUT

Figure 32. Shaft seal on propeller stuffing box may require repacking when it leaks. Gland nut is then tightened, followed by locknut.

Leaks, quite often, can also be caused by nothing more than a loose gland—when tightened, the leak will stop. The same thing can also happen on the stuffing box for a rudder post, with the same cure. If the leak doesn't stop in either place, the gland may have to be repacked with flax that comes in braided-rope form. When the old packing has been removed, the new material is packed around the shaft and the gland nut tightened down on it. Nylon seals are also available for this purpose. Persistent leaks after repacking should mean calling in a mechanic to trace and cure the problem.

SEACOCKS

A through-hull fitting should be used wherever there's an inlet for sea water on your boat. Most builders follow this practice faithfully but you occasionally find an inlet without a seacock. Where you do, have one installed or you'll have no way of stopping the flow in an emergency. It's a good idea to have a sketch showing the location of all the inlets on your boat so you can inspect them several times during the season. Look for leaks in the connections and make sure the flange nut is tight. On wooden hulls, check the screws in the mounting. Work the handle on the seacock to make sure it operates and hasn't frozen, as bronze will sometimes do, then lubricate the valve.

INSIDE-HULL HARDWARE ON SAILBOATS

This includes fittings like chainplate straps, anchors for shrouds and stays, keelbolts, etc. Look for cracks or corrosion that may have weakened the metal and check the fastenings to see they are tight. Where the keel boats are accessible, clean off the bilge dirt and tighten them. Fin keels should be checked when the boat is out of the water—look for any cracks in the joint with the hull. Shallow surface cracks can be filled in, but anything deeper warrants a thorough check of the keel bolts inside to make sure they are tight.

INSIDE HULL STRUCTURE: BULKHEADS, FLOORS, ETC.

While you're working below decks, give these parts of the framing some attention. In a fiberglass hull, the bulkheads and floors may be of wood and bonded in place with tape. In time, the joint can soften and the wood shift. These places can also develop dry rot if they're down in the bilge so check for both loose bonds and signs of rot. The floors in wooden hulls may also be trouble spots where the fastenings to the frames have corroded or loosened.

Any loose sections in cabin or deckhouse soles can be annoying and a hazard underfoot. Where the wood is badly warped, the section will never fit right so replace it. Loose sections can sometimes be tightened by gluing little strips of wood, called shims, onto the bottom where they bear on a floor or frame.

The Care of Bilge Pumps

Many a boat owner secretly wishes his bilges might be that dry he'd have to dust them instead of using a pump. Sad to say there's not much chance of that coming true, for most boats do need occasional pumping. Whether you rely on a portable pump, a trusty, hand-operated diaphragm model or an electric one, they all need maintenance in one form or another. And the flotsam that gets into the bilge—mud, rust, cigarette butts and what have you—adds to their care. Some of this debris can be kept out of the pump by putting a strainer in the inlet—you can get bronze ones to fit most hose sizes. There's also an in-line strainer with the filter element in a clear plastic case so you can see the dirt.

The Portables. The hand-operated piston type, like the so-called Navy model that can also be mounted on a bulkhead, is relatively easy to keep up. Debris may clog the valves but it can be removed by taking the pump apart. Replacements for the valves and other parts are available and it's a good idea to have some aboard.

Diaphragm Models. The simplest of these are the manual type which in spite of the large diameter of the intake and outlet valves, will get plugged up. To clean out the junk, break the hose connections and take the pump apart. Lubricate any moving parts after you clean it. The diaphragms will last a reasonably long time before replacement but it's also a good idea to keep a spare on hand.

The electric-powered diaphragm pumps require checking at the line connections for leaks and any servicing called for in the manual. Some, with a footvalve in the bilge for retaining the prime, should be inspected. Most of the pumps re-

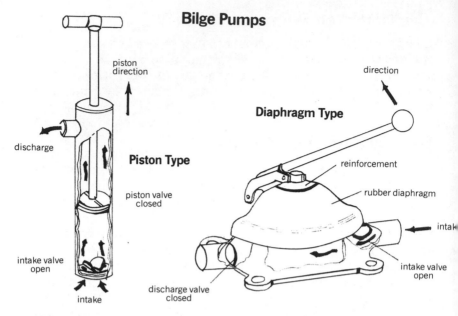

Bilge Pumps

piston direction

direction

Diaphragm Type

discharge

Piston Type

piston valve closed

reinforcement

rubber diaphragm

intake

intake valve open

intake valve open

intake

discharge valve closed

Figure 33.

quire some form of strainer in the line going to the pump that requires periodic cleaning.

Electric Bilge Pumps. These are usually installed at the lowest point in the bilge and will run completely under water. If the pump quits, look for debris wrapped around the impeller, and if the blockage has broken any blades put in a new impeller—an easy job to do. The wiring to these pumps is important as most of the time they're submerged. Any breaks in the insulation may cause a short circuit, so keep the wiring in good condition.

Upkeep of the Galley and Head

At the beginning of this section we compared the below-deck area on a boat to that of a spacecraft—a lot of living in a very little space. And this is nowhere more evident than in the galley and head. Though these facilities are not as critical to the boat's operation as the engines or sails, any breakdown is soon felt by everyone aboard.

Here is a quick rundown of what is normally done to keep the galley and head functioning smoothly:

PLUMBING

Out of sight and usually out of mind unless it starts leaking over the floor or fills up the bilge. Begin your work on the piping by checking as many of the lines and connections as you can reach, looking for any telltale dribbles. We covered the repair of water lines earlier in this section so if you have any problems, please go back to it.

If you've laid up the boat for the winter, the water system may have been filled with a non-toxic antifreeze which should be drained out and flushed before filling the system with fresh water. The same thing holds true for pressure water systems also covered earlier along with the maintenance of hot-water heaters.

THE HEAD

Probably the smallest stand-up compartment on a boat, the head often has all the room of a phone booth, so facilities are really crowded and hard to maintain. Earlier in this section under "Water Supply System", we covered the upkeep of the lines that feed the sink and shower (if any) in the head. Beside checking these, you should also look at the faucets, any shutoff valves, etc. for signs of leaks, replacing the washers or packing if needed.

Toilets. Keeping these in good working order is the most important part of maintenance in the head, even more so today because of the current U. S. Coast Guard regulations on marine sanitation devices. Briefly stated, it is now in violation of federal law (and with fines up to $2,000) to discharge raw sewerage from any vessel in U. S. waters within the 3 mile limit and in some areas any discharge is prohibited.

The regulations can be divided into two categories: boats 65′ in length or less and boats over 65′. All boats 65′ or less, regardless of when they were built, must now have a Type I, II, or III MSD (Marine Sanitation Device) installed as of 30

January 1980 or have no permanently installed toilet at all. The regulations do not include portable toilets that can be carried on or off the vessel. The only distinction made between new and existing boats is that the new boats had to have one of the three types installed starting 30 January 1977.

New boats over 65' should also have had one of the types installed by 1977 but if they don't have a Type I installed by 1980 they'll have to have a II or III. Existing boats over 65' don't have any regulations until January 1980, by which time they must have had a Type II or III. There's one exception here too: if a Type I was ordered by 30 January 1978 and installed by the same date in 1979, it can be used for the life of the device.

The Marine Sanitation Devices operate with either a treat and discharge system or a non-discharge device such as a holding tank or recirculating toilet system. The differences between Types I, II and III depend on the type of system used and the degree to which each treat the sewerage in reducing the fecal coliform count and solids. The discharge from a Type II is much "cleaner" than that of a Type I. Type IIIs are retention devices—holding tanks and recirculating devices.

Since both the Coast Guard regulations and any state or local laws on Marine Sanitation Devices may affect the operation of those on your boat you should be familiar with them. You can get copies of publication C. G. 485, on their regulations, from the nearest Coast Guard district office or Marine Safety Office, or by writing to: U. S. Coast Guard Headquarters, Commandant (G-WEP-3-TP-12), Washington, D. C. 20590. Your local, state or municipal government office should have information on any laws that may also require the use of these devices in your waters.

MANUAL TOILETS

In spite of the warning most owners post over the john, some neophyte to boating tosses in something it was never designed to take. Usually, the only way to fix this is to take the head apart and get out the culprit. There are some jobs you can do at annual upkeep time that will keep other troubles from developing.

Begin by pouring a detergent that also lubricates into the bowl of the john, pump it through to the parts inside, then flush it out. If any leaks develop, try tightening all the connections. If they persist, you may have to replace a broken valve or gasket. Most toilet manufacturers package a kit of needed replacement parts so keep one on on board. On electric toilets, make it a point to check the control switch and wiring for loose connections or signs of wear—replacing anything that needs it.

Figure 34. Waste treatment unit of sanitation system is in bilge, generates own disinfectant, requires periodic maintenance including adding salt when used in fresh water.

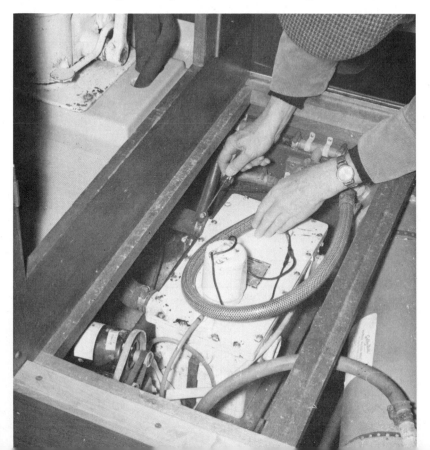

UPKEEP OF MARINE SANITATION DEVICES

With the variety of these devices in use on boats today, it would be impossible to cover the maintenance of them all. The best guide in keeping them up is to follow instructions in the service manuals that come with the units. In general, here are some checkpoints to keep in mind at annual maintenance time. Look at all the components (unless the unit is completely self-contained and they are not accessible) such as the pump, intake and discharge lines, connections, holding tank (including the venting) for any signs of leaks or broken parts. Some devices have a treatment system, (macerator/chlorinator) often below the floor in the head, that may require periodic cleaning, flushing and replacement of the chemicals—also check for any leaks here.

THE GALLEY

Another high activity area below decks with all facilities for food preparation, cooking and refrigeration concentrated in a small place. These are the jobs there that should be on your check list:

Supply Lines. Here again their upkeep was covered earlier in this section but make sure to go over the lines to the sink for any signs of leaks which should be repaired. And remember to do the drain line, trap and seacock at the outlet.

Valves And Fittings. If you didn't go over these before, check them for leaks especially in any shutoff valves below the sink that can develop a sneaky leak out of sight running into the bilge. The repair parts for most faucets and valves can be bought at a plumbing supply store.

Stoves. The upkeep of these largely depends on the type of fuel used—some requiring more maintenance than others. With liquid-fuel stoves, pressure from the pump is important, and the valves that control the flow to the burners must be kept clean. When you take the burners apart, remember the assembly order—some are a bit tricky to put back together. All fuel tanks should have a pressure gauge, relief valve and shutoff which should be closed when the stove is not in use. Another safety precaution is to have a metal drip pan with a ¾-inch lip on all sides under any stove that uses liquid fuel.

Propane or CNG (Compressed Natural Gas) Types. Care of these involves keeping the burners clean—using a fine wire in the orifices to do it. Make sure the mixing valve on each burner is admitting the right amount of air—too lean and the flame lacks heat, too much and it will soot the pots. Most owners with gas stoves close the shutoff valve on the supply line after each use. All stoves should be installed following the recommended practices of the ABYC (American Boat and Yacht Council), 190 Ketcham Ave., Amityville, N.Y. 11701, or similar ones of the NFPA (National Fire Protection Association), 60 Batterymarch St., Boston, Mass. 02110. Copies of their recommendations can be obtained by writing to these addresses.

Electric Stoves. Other than periodic cleaning, these require the least upkeep—almost nil. The wiring to the stove must be heavy enough to carry the wattage and kept in good condition. Problems with the shoreside power connection will usually show up when the stove is in use (and often in the middle of breakfast). Damage to the cable, plug or outlet should be repaired by a marine electrician or replaced.

Note: Do you have a fire extinguisher within easy reach of, though not behind, the stove? If not, play it safe and install one.

REFRIGERATORS AND FREEZERS

There are several different types of refrigeration systems used on boats today. The most common is probably the mechanical compression system, and where there's space for the unit to work efficiently, builders will install fridges and freezers similar to their household cousins ashore. Since the compressor in most of these is a factory-sealed, air-cooled unit, they require little upkeep other than periodic cleaning of the condenser and checking the temperature inside the box. Where air cooling isn't practical, the compressor may be cooled by sea water with a pump and through-hull fittings on the intake and discharge connections which require maintenance. The mechanical unit may be below the box or if space is tight, installed in the bilge.

Eutectic (Holding Plate) Systems. Used on auxiliary sailboats and in the galleys of trawlers and cruising powerboats, the advantage of this refrigeration is that the holding plate can be frozen solid with only a few hours running of the engine. Eutectics use the same cycle as a mechanical compression system but drive the compressor through a magnetic clutch on the engine. The condenser is sea water cooled by the pump on the block. This auxiliary equipment needs some upkeep—checking the compressor belt for wear, for leaks in the connections on the sea-water line, seacocks, etc.

Thermoelectric Type. The disadvantage of these refrigerators is they're not very efficient and the boxes are small—2 cubic feet and under. Since they have no moving parts, they require no maintenance.

PERSONAL FLOTATION DEVICES (LIFE PRESERVERS)

Your maintenance work should include inspecting all life jackets, vests, buoyant cushions, etc. stowed below. Here are some questions to ask yourself about them:

- Do I have enough on board to meet U. S. Coast Guard Regulations?
- Are they of the approved and acceptable types?
- When was the last time they were inspected?
- Do I remember to tell everyone who comes aboard where they are kept?

(Some owners clearly label the storage spaces with small signs.)

Your check of PFD's should include the webbing and fabric (for signs of deterioration that could weaken them) and of the material inside (feeling it for signs of crumbling). With so many children a part of boating life today, it's a good idea to have child-size life jackets on hand.

FIRE EXTINGUISHERS

Still in the "safety" department of the upkeep below, these are another "must" item on your list. Have enough extinguishers to meet the Coast Guard requirements for your length boat (four classes) and whether or not there is a fixed extinguishing system in the "machinery space" (presumably the engine compartment). The requirements also depend on the agent used to control the fire—CO_2, dry chemicals or Freon.

Location of the extinguishers is also a factor—have the right type easily accessible to fight the kind of fire most frequent in the space being protected. In addition to portables, some owners have a fixed or so-called "blanket" system installed in the engine and/or fuel tank spaces.

In maintaining portable extinguishers, check the pressure gauge every six months, and test them at least once during the season. See that each one has a tag with a record of the last charge and inspection dates. Fixed systems are more complex to service and should be done by a specialist at whatever interval the service manual shows. For more information on fire-protection equipment, you can get the recommended standards for motor craft from the NFPA.

BONDING SYSTEM

It's been reported that some new owners have never heard of this and don't know there is such a system on their boat. Though out of sight down in the hull, the system is important for safety. The wiring connects equipment like the engine, auxiliary generator, metal tanks, seacocks, etc. to a copper ground plate on the outside of fiberglass and wooden hulls. Metal hulls act as their own ground plate. The bonding system dissipates any static electricity charge that may collect in the equipment and prevents an accidental spark from exploding gasoline vapors in the bilge.

Keeping up the system involves inspecting the connections to make sure they are tight with no breaks in the wire and that it is above the normal bilge-water level. The outside ground plate should be checked for signs of corrosion and on a wooden hull, dry rot beneath it.

DRY ROT SEARCH

This fungus that attacks the wooden parts of a boat was described in the first section, but it's important enough to make it a must item in your upkeep work below. When you're working there, be on the alert for any signs of the rot—a stale, musty smell, damp, spongy spots, peeling paint, discolored brightwork, etc. Many owners think dry rot is only found in a wooden hull but as we said earlier the fungus can attack the wooden parts in a fiberglass or metal hull as well. Look for it behind joinerwork, backs of panels and locker doors, bottoms of bulkheads and other spots. In many cases, the damage isn't discovered until it's worked through to the surface. Keep alert and search for it whenever you're working below. One way to help prevent it on any boat is by adequate ventilation, which we'll cover later.

Cabin and Deckhouse Interiors

With the mechanical maintenance below completed, and all the dirty work that goes along with it, you can turn whatever energy you have left to the living space fondly called home. You spend a great deal of time there so give it some tender, loving care. This is what is usually involved:

THE REMOVABLE FURNISHINGS

Today's trend of making boat interiors resemble those of homes ashore means that furnishings, such as chairs, convertible sofas, lamps, tables, etc., can often be taken off for professional refurbishment. This will also give you more working room for doing any painting or varnishing in the cabin or deckhouse. At the same time, the first mate will have an option to change the decorative scheme.

DRAPES, CUSHIONS, MATTRESSES AND BEDDING

These can get pretty seedy-looking too, so bring any ashore that can stand a spruceup or replacement. Most of these are custom-made to fit the interior so there may be a long lead time involved. To remove dirt on built-in cushions and upholstery, use one of the foam-type cleaners.

When your boat has been laid up for storage, you may find mould and mildew on many of the surfaces below decks where the spores attach themselves to almost anything. To take off the coating on fabrics, spray on a chemical mildew-remover; on durable surfaces use a weak solution of bleach, testing first to be sure it doesn't take out the color. Better ventilation of the interior will help prevent this, and we'll go into this later in this section.

INTERIOR PAINT AND BRIGHTWORK

The first job in keeping this up is to wash all painted surfaces with a mild detergent, followed by rinsing and drying. Repeat the treatment on the brightwork but use a milder solution. For teak trim, one of the restorers will clean and bring back the natural color. Where the finish on panelling is still good, a household furniture polish that cleans and waxes can often restore the color and lustre. If the old varnish is dull, all it may need is a light sanding and a new coat to keep it in good condition.

When you decide to go the whole route and completely refinish the interior, some prep work may be needed first. Fill in any nicks and scratches in the paint. The stained color of most brightwork can be matched with a colored-wax crayon to touch up surface marks. To help in choosing finishes for the interior, use the Paint Chart at the end of the first section. The tips on painting and varnishing that follow it are also useful.

MAKING THE INTERIOR MORE LIVABLE

Finding a place to stow everything that's needed on a cruise is a perennial problem on most boats, especially the smaller ones. While you're at the maintenance work below is a good time to help solve it by adding built-ins that use wasted space and add comfort and convenience.

For example, racks can be installed over the berths in a forward stateroom, shelves added below the sink in a head and openings cut below dinette seats to provide more storage lockers. Improvements like these are well within the capability of anyone handy with tools.

Ventilation Below Decks

Apart from the obvious reasons of safety and health, an adequate supply of fresh, clean air is important in the maintenance of any boat below decks. Good circulation there will help prevent dry rot in the hull, stop corrosion of the equipment and keep mould and mildew from interior surfaces, charts and clothing.

HOW VENTILATION WORKS

To most owners, ventilation means the circulation of air below decks, but an engineer thinks of it as so many air exchanges in the ventilated space, the number depending on its usage. The air flow to produce these exchanges is due to the difference in pressure inside and outside the space. On a boat, it's done two ways as the drawing shows:

1. NATURAL VENTILATION

This comes from the wind at anchor or air movement under way. Hatches, ports and ventilators admit the air and channel the flow below to exhaust foul air and noxious fumes. In problem areas such as the galley, head or a forward stateroom, the flow can be stepped up by installing ventilators, such as the Dorade type, on sailboats, mush-

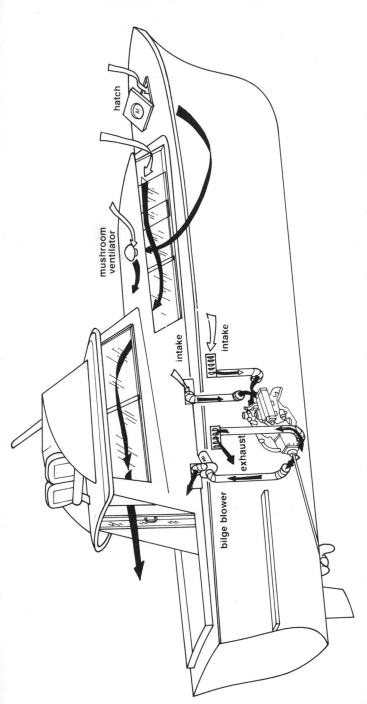

hatch

mushroom
ventilator

intake

intake

bilge blower

exhaust

Figure 35. Ventilation on typical cruiser. Natural system is from air flow when under way or wind at anchor. Powered system uses mechanical blower to bring fresh air below decks and exhaust fumes and gasoline vapors.

rooms (with low height for cabin tops) and flexible, plastic snap-in models on decks. Small ventilating hatches can also be installed where practical.

The engine compartment on boats is a critical area for ventilation because of gas fumes trapped in the bilge. As we mentioned earlier, the Coast Guard rules make it mandatory to have natural as well as powered ventilation in this space.

The natural air flow on a sailboat can be increased by rigging an adjustable windsail over a hatch to scoop some of the breeze below. For anyone with a sewing machine, these are fairly easy to make of nylon, Dacron or canvas or they can be bought ready-made. A sailmaker can turn out a custom-tailored one. The same trick will also work if there is some way of rigging the windsail over a hatch on a powerboat.

2. POWERED VENTILATION

This type of air flow comes from intake openings and ducts that bring it below decks where it is exhausted by mechanical blowers through ventilators or louvers. The air exchange can also come from combination ventilators with motor-driven fans inside.

A powered ventilation system is vital to the engine compartment. The Coast Guard regulations specify minimum blower capacities, based on compartment volume and the size and location of exhaust ducts. Where a ventilation problem is suspected in the engine area, the cause should be determined and corrected—the best time to do it is while you're working below. The answer may be the exhaust-duct pickups are not down far enough in the bilge to suck out the fumes. As nearly as possible, they should be *below the engine* but above the normal bilge water level. Not enough blower capacity may be another cause and putting in a higher-rated model or even adding another duct and blower to the system could solve the problem.

VENTILATION IN LIVING SPACES

Quite often the difficulty in ventilating a cabin or deckhouse is not because of insufficient flow from outside but because of poor air circulation inside. This can help create a stale, musty odor that no amount of air freshening will dispel. Again, the best time to remedy this situation is when you're doing the maintenance below decks.

To increase the air flow between compartments, you can install midget louvers in bulkheads or cut in ventilating grilles which take a bit more work to put in. All below-berth spaces should be vented as well as cabinets, drawers, under-sink spaces, etc. Ventilating the bilges is more of a problem today with the current vogue of overall floor carpeting. Some builders get air below it by cutting openings in the bottoms of lockers and cabinets. This can be done by anyone handy with tools or by the yard. Sailboat purists often have gratings in the cabin sole to keep the bilges "sweet and clean" as the old seamen used to say. Again, this could be a "do-it-yourself" project.

FOREPEAK AND SAIL LOCKER

Often one of the forgotten spaces in the hull, this area should be on your inspection and upkeep list when you're working below. It needs the adequate ventilation we talked about earlier to prevent condensation that can produce corrosion and mildew of the gear stored there.

Where the space is used as a sail locker, the bags should be stowed on racks to keep them dry. The same thing is true for awnings and cockpit covers that often wind up on the bottom of everything. If you keep ground tackle up in the "eyes of the ship," give it a periodic check for any signs of corrosion on the metal. This should be sanded off and the spots primed and painted. Cordage too should be examined for wear and fraying. A rack at the bottom of the forepeak over the bilges will help in stowing gear and also keep the anchor rode dry and ready for use.

4. Layup and Storage

Depending on the length of the season and the area of the country, many boats are laid up for storage. In colder climates this is done to protect them from damage by freezing temperatures. In the Sun Belt, owners store their boats if they're going north for the summer to safeguard them from hurricanes and keep them free of marine growth. Whatever the reason, this section of the guide will cover the work that is normally done in laying up a boat for storage.

The nature of this will vary, depending on where you do your boating and the kind of storage you choose—on land, in backyard, boatyard, or in the water as more skippers are doing north and south (depending on whether the boat can be left outdoors or needs protection inside). The choice is yours so we'll spell out the options along with their pros and cons later in this section.

For the actual layup, we'll outline the work generally done on the hull, the topsides and below decks to keep your boat in good condition during storage and ready for launching when it's over. Though you may not have the expertise for all the jobs or care to tackle some, they're a good checklist of what most capable yards and marinas do in preparing both power- and sailboats for storage.

Incidentally, though you mightn't think of it this way, when you lay up the boat you're also doing some of the fitting out she'll need before going back in the water. By getting more of the work done before storage, you'll have a chance to spend more time on your boat next season instead of beneath it.

Plan Early

You can't really do this for the layup too soon. The time to start is well in advance, at least several weeks before haulout. Give the choice of storage method serious consideration, weighing all the factors involved. If you decide on yard storage, advance planning is even more important. In populated areas where space is tight canvas all possible places. We'll outline what to look for in a marina later in this section.

Earlier in the book, we mentioned having a work schedule for maintenance and if you ever needed one, it's for all the jobs that have to be done at layup. To speed up the work, divide it into the "do-it-myself" and "let-the-yard-handle-it" categories and be realistic about your own skills—don't overrate them. Often a pro from the yard gang can do a better job faster and in the long run at less cost. It may also help to go over your tool inventory to see if everything's there to handle the work you plan. An investment in power tools pays dividends because it makes the jobs easier and quicker. Also, service manuals for the equipment aboard are a must when you're laying up the boat. We'll cover what is usually done on engines, cooling and water systems, plumbing, etc., but the work varies among manufacturers so have the manuals on hand for specifics.

The Storage Options

In deciding which of these is best for you, the most important factor is obviously what is available in your area within
the limits dictated by climate and the method that offers the
most protection for your boat. For example, dry storage in the
South will require protection from the sun, but equipment
doesn't need winterizing. In the north, wet storage may offer
some advantages over that on land, but a bubble or other
de-icing system is needed to stop ice formation and damage
to the hull. Indoor storage has some advantages, but in
crowded boating areas there may not be any available.

Beyond local availability, there are other factors to keep in
mind. The size and weight of your boat is one—smaller boats
can be carried on a trailer, opening up the possibility of
doing the hauling and storing yourself in your backyard. A
good-sized sailboat with a tall rig may require a travelling
lift for the haulout and a crane to unstep the mast if it's to
be stored on the ground. Smaller boats lend themselves to
stack storage, offering immediate accessibility for launching
when the season begins. And last but not least, is the budget
you've set for the work. A slim one may mean doing most of
the work yourself. With a healthy exchequer you can have a
yard do the layup but you'll miss all the joy of "messing
about," as the Water Rat said.

BACKYARD STORAGE

Let's begin with this option for if your boat can be hauled
and stored on a trailer, it's the simplest and cheapest method.
Before you go gung-ho for it though, here are some points to
consider:

On the plus side, it's the most accessible kind of storage—
the boat is right on your doorstep so to speak, secure against
theft and convenient to work on at any time. And if you have
a home workshop, these facilities can help with the maintenance. You should have a good location for the trailer—a
well-drained spot far enough away from other buildings so

there's no fire risk if you have onboard gas tanks. Will the boat be an eyesore to the neighbors? A 30-footer stored in the driveway all winter is not always an asset to the neighborhood. And the whine of a power saw at night may not make any friends for you either.

When you store on your property, will the tax man enter the picture? In many places he does, so better check. Also what kind of insurance do you need? Will your homeowner's policy cover the boat and for how much liability? Your broker should have the answer.

Should you elect the backyard storage route, think about the job of hauling out and keeping the boat on a trailer. If it can be loaded from a marina ramp, reserve a time slot—it can be a busy place on weekends at the end of the season. Before you haul the boat, try to get as much weight off as possible not only to reduce the load on the rig but to avoid stresses on the hull during storage. Take off heavy equipment like big outboards, the outside sterndrive unit if you can, and any removable gear that adds weight.

When you park the trailer, take the weight off the tires by jacking up the frame so they clear the ground. Put concrete blocks or heavy timbers under the axles and use sleepers on the ground so supports don't settle. If the outside sterndrive unit or a big outboard can't be taken off the boat, shore up the lowest points to take the strain of their weight off the hull.

Some hulls are difficult to load and cradle on a trailer, deep-keel sailboats may require special supports or a crane to lift them on the trailer. Some yards will do this, of course for a charge, and reverse the process at launching time. You can also rent husky trailers that will carry fairly heavy boats. In using them, think about the kind of hitch needed for towing and the strain the rig may put on your car's transmission. The saving in storage costs may not be worth a repair bill if anything breaks down.

If the trailer act is not your dish of tea, you can still store the boat in your backyard by having a service company in your area haul the boat and load it on a flatbed trailer. They'll neatly deposit it wherever you want it and then reverse the routine at the start of the new season.

Whenever a boat is stored outside, it usually needs some

form of cover with a supporting framework to protect it. To prevent condensation, the cover must have ventilation built-in. We'll get into all of these later in this section.

Finally, after you've turned over in your mind all the factors about the backyard/trailer approach, get out your pocket calculator and run up the total cost. Compare it with an estimate of what a yard will charge for the haulout and storage. The saving may not be enough to justify doing the work yourself.

BOATYARD STORAGE

For years this has been the traditional way of storing boats, especially in winter climates where ice can damage the hull. This picture is changing today as newer methods come in; but yard storage still offers advantages not only in colder parts of the country but in warmer waters as well.

If you decide to store your boat in a yard, try to get the answers to the following questions before you make a commitment, particularly if you're a newcomer to boating or to the yard or marina:

- Is it accessible and within easy driving distance of your home? (You may be bushed working on the boat and not relish a long trip.)
- How close to high tide are the boats—any danger of flooding?
- Do they have equipment to handle your boat safely?
- How good is the security during the off-season—someone responsible there, watchman on during the night, risk of pilferage?
- Fire protection—hydrants in the yard, wide lanes for equipment to get in, plowed in winter?
- Enough working room around the boats—well blocked and shored, free of junk and debris that can start fires?
- Do they have capable professionals to do the work—backed by shops?
- What are the charges for hauling and storage—hourly labor rates?
- How much work can you do yourself? Some yards have

rules that restrict this, others require all supplies to be
bought there.
- Insurance—does the yard cover for fire and theft? Many
  don't, so check your broker on your own coverage during
  storage.
- Their reputation—what do boat owners who use the yard
  think of them—any nixies on service, handling, prices
  too high, etc.?
- Service contract—if there is one, read and understand
  the fine print before you sign and make a commitment.

If you're happy with the answers to these questions, and
maybe willing to compromise on a few doubtful ones, try to
get a firm date on the haulout time. Later on after you know
what professional help you may need on the layup, check
back with the management so you can get in early on their
work schedule. At the same time, try to give them a "guesti-
mate" on when you'd like your boat back in the water. It may
seem like a long time off, but it can help with the yard's space
allocation and get you afloat sooner at the new season.

DRY OR WET STORAGE?

At one time the most popular way, and often the only one,
to store a boat was to take it out of the water and keep it on
land—the dry storage method. True, some boats were left in
warmer waters but for a vast majority in colder climates, the
danger of ice damage to the hull left no other choice. Today
that picture is rapidly changing with the advent of bubble
systems and other methods that keep ice from forming—
more owners are keeping their boats afloat. In many areas,
boatyards and marinas offer both dry and wet storage in
their facilities. And there are other places where you can lay
up a boat in the water, as we'll point out later on. But for now,
let's take a look at the pros and cons of both dry and wet
storage for your consideration.

DRY STORAGE

This method has been used for so many years that some

owners feel it's the only way to store a boat. They like having it out of the water and being able to work on the hull. When it is well protected with a cover, there isn't as much likelihood of condensation forming inside as there would be afloat. Getting in and out of the hull and carrying everything needed with you is a bit of nuisance on land but still easier than doing it on the water. With the boat ashore, there is also the fringe benefit of the camaraderie of other skippers, kindred spirits, enjoying the spring ritual of fitting out.

In the hurricane belt, land storage offers freedom from worry about a blow damaging the boat if it's afloat. This can be a nail-biting experience if the owner is in the North and his boat is miles away in the South. Land storage also offers freedom from worry about marine growth that can foul the bottom in a shorter time in warmer waters.

OUTDOOR OR INSIDE DRY STORAGE?

In some places, this is an additional option in laying up a boat. Outdoors is almost always cheaper than storage in a shed or building which is often at a premium and on a priority basis with old customers getting first chance at any vacant space. Old salts preferred storing a boat outside since they felt it reduced shrinking of the planking because of the natural humidity in the air. However, in warmer climates outdoor storage under a hot sun can discolor the gel coat on a fiberglass boat and warp wooden topside surfaces unless it is well protected.

In comparing both outside and inside storage, there are some goodies going with the inside route, though it costs more. Inside storage keeps fiberglass and metal hulls in better condition—less fading of the glass mentioned previously with outdoor storage and less chance of rust and corrosion of metal hulls. Also, you probably won't need a cover with the boat inside. Another plus is being able to work regardless of the weather, thus having greater protection when painting and varnishing. Security too, should be better inside a building if it's locked and checked by a night watchman.

On inside storage, insurance may enter the picture, so

check on your coverage there—there is a risk of fire spreading more quickly. The location of your boat inside can also be a factor if you're in a hurry to have it in the water. The usual rule is "First In—Last Out" and you may have to wait. Also on the debit side with inside storage is the obvious one that with a sailboat, the mast will have to be unstepped, often at additional cost. However, if it's taken out and stored on the ground the upkeep work is easier to do.

WET STORAGE

We gave this as an option before but if you're considering it for winter storage, here's what makes it possible for colder parts of the country. The way to stop ice from forming around a boat hull is to circulate warm water from the bottom with a de-icing (bubble) system as most boatyards and marinas do in their wet storage. The bubbles come from holes in a pipe on the bottom fed by an air compressor ashore. As they rise to the top, they bring up warm water and prevent the ice from forming. The same thing can be done mechanically using a propeller or pump on the bottom, driven by a submersible electric motor. This is much less expensive, making it feasible for use by an individual owner, or within a bigger system, for several boats rafted together.

Like most of the other options we outlined, there are credits and debits on the wet storage approach. Here are some you should take into account:

- *Location.* Check this out not only from the land side but from the water as well. Is the mooring or dockside protected from storms, free of strong currents, waste pollution, sewerage, etc.?
- *Security.* How much is there? Someone to check on the de-icing system and fix it in case of breakdown?
- *Convenience.* Will you be able to do the layup and fitting-out work there? The boat will still have to be hauled for hull work, bottom painting, etc.
- *Insurance.* Can your broker cover against fire and theft there?

Figure 36. Dry storage in a boatyard is still the most popular method in colder climates, and offers some advantages to the owners.

Figure 37. The ultimate in winter layup. Inside storage is more expensive but offers better protection and a chance to get an early start on fitting-out.

Figure 38. Wet storage at a marina. Growing use of de-icing systems makes storage afloat practical in colder climates. Note bubbles from de-icer in water below front of dock.

- *Cover.* It will have to be well braced and fastened against wind and storms—more exposed than on land.
- *Sailboats.* The rigging and spars will take more of a beating afloat unless they're taken out and stored ashore.
- *Wooden Hulls.* A plus here because the planking won't dry out. A minus too: teredos can do their dirty work, especially in warmer waters.
- *Metal Hulls.* A debit due to corrosion and possible damage from galvanic action.
- *All Hulls.* Wet storage means less strain on them from lifting, cradles and shores—the hull is evenly supported.
- *Marine Growth.* A minus unless the storage is in fresh water. In salt, bottom growth may require antifouling paint.
- *Underwater Hull Hardware.* The same problem as with metal hulls.
- *Condensation.* More likely to cause damage from dry rot and corrosion inside the hull. Ventilation is a must.
- *Total Cost.* How does it compare with land storage? Enough of a saving to make the wet route worthwhile?

WET STORAGE IN FRESH WATER

It may come as news to some owners that in some parts of the country you can store your boat in fresh water. Some yards and marinas are close enough to a creek or pond so boats can be hauled out in salt water and moved into fresh water. They also may offer under-cover wet storage, a plus in the Sun Belt.

PRIVATE WET STORAGE

Where you live on protected water and are lucky enough to keep your boat there, the possibility opens up of doing your own wet storage. Even in cold climates you can keep the water from freezing around the hull with the submerged propeller system we described before. This system can also be used if you can find space at a yacht club (some have their own bubble systems, too) or another protected location. Several owners can band together and keep their boats in a snug spot using a common de-icing system.

STACK STORAGE

Still another option that combines the merits of dry storage with the advantages of being under cover, provided, your boat is within the size limits of the system. This involves a big forklift to pick up the boats alongside a dock, carry them to the stack for storage in cubbyholes. Stacks offer both transient and off-season storage. At most places you can phone in the time you want your boat so when you arrive it's in the water, ready to go.

The layup work, such as winterizing inboard engines and other preparation chores, must be done before the boat is stored in a stack for any period of time. Most users prefer to cover their boats because only the stack tops are covered, and sun and dirt can still affect the boats.

Before Hauling Out

With a firm date set for this, try to get as much removable equipment and loose gear off the boat as possible—sails, clothing, food that will spoil, life preservers, ground tackle, outboard motor, etc. Also take off anything that can be affected during storage such as electronics, cooking fuel tanks, fire extinguishers for recharging. Having these ashore offers an opportunity to check their condition and have any repairs made during storage. It will also provide more working room in the boat for layup jobs, reduce the risk of theft and help improve ventilation under a winter cover. Remember though to keep aboard whatever is needed for the run to the yard if you're storing there.

These are general suggestions that will help make the layup easier; but there are also some specifics to keep in mind depending on the storage method used. In the trailer/ backyard approach, the main idea in removing equipment is to reduce the weight on the rig and stress on the hull in storage as we pointed out before.

When you're storing in a yard, make sure your cradle is

available and in good condition. See if it needs any new supports or tightening of the fastenings. Lacking a cradle at hand, the yard might jockey the boat on temporary blocking and let it stay there during the storage period.

Masts, Spars and Rigging—In or out?

If sail is your love, these should get special attention at layup and storage time. Some yards and marinas will unstep the mast and store it separately, others will haul the boat with it standing. Taking out the mast gives you a chance to work on it and the standing rigging while they're on the ground—a lot easier than doing it aloft. We'll go into the layup of tophamper later on.

On sailboats with sloop or cutter rig, the unstepped mast is often laid in x-frames and used as the strongback or ridgepole of the frame for the winter cover. If you do this, the spreaders and shrouds should come off and either cover the winches or take them off the mast. This way you can go over the winches during storage and clean and lubricate them.

At some yards, masts and spars are stored in a spar loft.

Figure 39. Spar loft at a yard offers protected storage for masts, spars and rigging—a must for wooden spars and good for aluminum ones, too.

There aren't too many of these left but if you can find one, use it. Under-cover storage is a must for wooden spars as protection against weathering and warping. The place should be dry with the spars laid on enough supports for their length with any related rigging alongside. Too many yards today store spars on outside racks or just on top of saw horses with only a flimsy plastic covering to protect them. Alloy masts and spars don't need as much protection as wooden ones, but it's still wiser to keep them under some form of durable cover.

On the rigging, have the yard carefully tag and coil everything with the name of your boat on it—there's usually a tangle of wires and fittings during storage, and there's a hassle sorting it out at fitting-out time. Though the yard will store it, many owners take their running rigging home to inspect it and replace any worn cordage, damaged blocks and fittings.

Cleaning the Bottom

We went around the track on this before in the first section as part of the annual maintenance, but if you're laying up the boat it's just as important. Any delay in getting off the bottom growth will make the job that much harder. Two hours is about the limit—anything after that causes the growth to harden like cement; nothing short of blasting will get it off.

Most yards include bottom cleaning as part of their haul-out and storage charge; if they do it with steam, it's a better job. While the boat is in the slings, make sure the crew shift the sling and cleans underneath. Some yards rent high-pressure cleaning machines for do-it-yourself owners. These work well but glasses should be worn as the chemical spray can injure the eyes.

Lacking any power methods, a creditable job can still be done—*if it is tackled quickly,* using a stiff brush, hose and plenty of elbow grease. Work from the boot stripe down, using a scraper with a dulled edge (a husky pancake turner works, too). But use care particularly on fiberglass so you don't dig into the gel coat. A nylon scrub pad, crumbled screening, or whatever you can improvise, will help if the growth is still soft. One of the liquid, non-scrubbing algae removers can be used to work over any stubborn spots. Getting the bottom clean on a wooden hull is a must if you want to use antifouling paint for protection during storage.

USE CARE IN SANDING

This can be left until later but the experts recommend sanding the bottom as soon as it's dry after cleaning—the old paint will still be a bit soft and easier to bring down to a smooth finish. Before you tackle the job, put on a mask, hat and safety glasses. The dust from sanding the old paint can be toxic, irritating the eyes and getting in your hair. Use the right-size grit for the job—the flexible, strip gadgets or silicon-carbide metal discs in a power drill may help. Belt sanders take off paint fast but running on the edges will gouge the surface. The carborundum cloth that floor sanding companies use works well in a belt sander.

When you're doing the sanding, don't take off any paint that may be on the underwater hardware—struts, ground plate, etc. This protects it from galvanic corrosion and the same thing holds true for zinc anodes but in reverse. Don't paint over them or you'll lose their protection.

REPAIRING BOTTOM DAMAGE

With the old paint off, give the surface a careful inspection for any damaged spots—sprung planks, loose caulking or fastenings, dry rot, etc.—on wooden hulls. On glass and metal hulls look for cracks, digs and dents. Mark the places with crayon for repairing before you put on a layup coat of bottom paint on wooden hulls, or for later attention at fitting-out time. For these repairs, see Section 1.

PRIMING THE BOTTOM

We mentioned this for wooden hulls before and the reason some owners do it is to keep the seam caulking from drying out during storage. The paint also acts as a bond-primer for the final bottom coat before the boat is put in the water. If

Figure 40. Loose fastenings in a wooden hull should be tightened or replaced at layup. These were found under a copper ground plate.

Figure 41. Cradle for deep keel boat is well braced with good support. Note long pad at top of shores that fits underbody at bilge.

you're doing it, use a light prime coat for storage protection, but make sure it is compatible with the old coating. The Paint Chart at the end of the first section will help you pick a finish.

Wet storage, especially in warmer waters, is another case where the bottom needs protection before any layup. The reason here is to stop marine growth from forming when the boat is left in the water. The same preparation as for a wooden hull should be completed and then a heavy coat of antifouling paint laid on. The underwater hardware should be protected against galvanic corrosion during wet storage by using one of the special paints for this purpose. Paints with a metallic inhibitor can actually cause this form of corrosion if used on the hardware to stop marine growth.

Cradles, Blocking and Shores

Some pros at the yards will tell you that more damage can happen to the hull from a badly-built cradle or improper blocking, than from several seasons of hard cruising or sailing. Unless the hull is properly supported, it may be sprung out of shape and weakened structurally when the boat gets in the water. Here is a rundown on the main points to watch when a yard puts up the boat on land or to follow if you do the job yourself.

CRADLES

The builder usually provides a shipping cradle for his product but some of these may need strengthening when they're used for storage. For small- to medium-size boats, a cradle of husky timbers shaped to fit the underbody will generally give sufficient support. On sailboats with a deep hull, fin keel or spade rudder, the cradle should follow the underbody closely, particularly along the bilges. The drawback with most powerboat hulls is there's usually not enough room under the cradle to work on the bottom, so if you're having a new one built, keep this in mind.

It makes good sense to keep your cradle in top condition and to have your boat's name on it in BIG LETTERS so it is available when the season is over. A yard will sometimes fork-lift all the cradles on the place into a big pile after the boats are launched—this is bad medicine. Try to see that yours is kept separate and undamaged. A boat should never be supported only by steel jackscrews during storage, or the old trick of using empty oil drums that you sometimes see. Both methods can damage the hull.

BLOCKING AND SHORES

These are often used where a cradle is not available or for one reason or another, impractical to support the hull. With this method, blocks are first placed under the keel at bow and stern, then intermediate ones are spaced along its length so the waterline of the boat is level. By setting up wedges under the blocks, the wedges can be eased out and the blocks shifted to paint the bottom beneath them. The blocks at the center of the keel shouldn't be higher than those at the bow and stern or the hull may become "hogged"—sprung enough out of shape to change the sheer.

While blocking supports the keel, shores keep the hull erect. These should rest on ground timbers to prevent their settling; and to spread the load over the planking, pads are used on top of the shores. The shores should never run to the underside of the sheer moulding or rub strake. They may push up the sheer and start leaks in the joint between deck and hull. Boats with a long overhang at bow and stern should have shores beneath them for support. When a hull has very little deadrise such as on shallow v-bottoms or houseboats where the aft sections are sometimes almost flat, the blocks and shores must be carefully placed to avoid any damage. It's a wise precaution to check all hull supports during storage to see they haven't shifted or settled. This can happen in colder climates when the ground thaws out.

Overall Washdown

By now this may be an old story from reading Section 1 on hull care which assumed the washdown was part of the annual maintenance, to be quickly followed by paint at fitting-out time. In laying up a boat for storage, the cleaning is equally important for if the dirt and chemicals aren't removed they have a long time to work into the finish and damage it. Salt spray and the air pollution today will attack most exposed surfaces on a boat and the condensation under a winter cover will compound it.

Before you begin the cleandown job, get off as much of the removable topsides gear as possible to have a clear field for the job. Begin at the highest point and work your way right down to the keel. Try to pick a warm day with low humidity so everything will dry quickly.

Laying Up The Hull

Begin the work here by draining the bilges, checking the fittings for any signs of corrosion or damage when you open them. It's also a good time to clean out the bilges using one of the chemical preparations on the market and a hose to flush them out. If there's a lot of dirt and grease, use the soaking method by filling the bilges with water until the grease dissolves, then flushing them out with a hose. Sponge up any water left after the cleaning so it doesn't freeze and damage the hull.

THE TOPSIDES

The hull above the waterline can take a beating during the season not only from sun and sea but from scraping on docks and from the chemicals in polluted waters. In fiberglass all it may need is a good cleaning with the agents we mentioned earlier, followed by waxing and polishing before the new season. Where the gel coat has lost its original lustre and been painted, a light sanding and fresh paint may be all that's required to put it back in condition. Repairs for more serious problems with the glass are covered in the first section of the book.

In wooden hulls, check the topsides for sprung planks, loose fastenings or caulking, and symptoms of dry rot. Aluminum and steel hulls should also be inspected for surface damages, dents and corrosion. Repairs for these problems are also covered in Section 1.

The brightwork on all hulls can become weathered so the varnish is gone exposing the wood. Unless this is covered, the grain will raise and the wood darken during storage, especially from the condensation under a cover. To protect it, give it a light sanding and a coat of varnish. Some form of protection is also needed for the topsides of boats left afloat in wet storage where there is greater exposure than on land. If you're going this route, give fiberglass topsides several heavy coats of wax and paint wooden or metal hulls.

UNDERWATER HULL HARDWARE

Protecting metal in this from galvanic corrosion is the job of sacrificial anodes or "zincs" as already explained. These come in the form of collars for shafts, tabs on rudders, blocks or plates, etc. A rough rule of thumb is one 4″ × 18″ standard zinc or its equivalent in area for every four feet of waterline length. On the layup, check the deterioration of the zincs and if they need replacing or beefing up with more anodes, make a note of the type and size you'll need.

On powerboat hulls, begin your inspection of the hardware at the transom, checking the trim tabs for corrosion, broken parts or loose fastenings. Give the rudders the same going over, then check the props for broken or bent blades which may need reconditioning in a shop during the storage period. Look at the shaft bearings for signs of wear and the struts for corrosion or loose fastenings. Work forward on the bottom, cleaning the intake screens and seacocks. Where there's a ground plate, check it for corrosion and the transducer for any signs of damage.

Sailboat hulls may have similar hardware which should get the same treatment. On spade rudders, check the condition of the fittings for corrosion or broken parts and do the same for deep-keel rudders. Outside chainplates are another hardware item to be gone over at layup as well as the fittings for jib and back stays. Where all these parts are on a wooden hull, look for signs of dry rot under the metal.

After you've laid up the engine on your boat which involves turning it over for certain jobs, wrap up the hull hardware work by sealing the exhaust pipes to keep out moisture and roaming wild life (yard mice are persistent).

OUTSIDE STERNDRIVE LAYUP

The normal maintenance work on these was described in the first section of this guide, but here are the salient points along with any specialized care for winterizing the unit. (Layup of the inside unit will be covered later.) Remember to use the service manual for the specifics.

1. Before you do any work on the unit remove the key from the ignition and take off the propeller as safety precautions.
2. Clean off the marine growth and any rust or grease your overall washdown may have missed. Use scrapers and wire brushes carefully to avoid damaging the paint. If you're storing the boat afloat and any paint is missing, use one of the special types on the unit to stop marine growth.
3. Check the entire unit for damaged or loose parts. Tighten those that need it—add any replacements to your order list.
4. Drain all the water and clean out all passages you can reach with a long wire. Vacuum out the deposits. Clean the intake screen.
5. Backwash the cooling system using a flushing hose adapter—some are built in. Drain out all the water to keep it from freezing.
6. Drain the oil in the housing, both upper and lower levels on some units. Check the color for water contamination (it usually turns a light brown). This may mean a cracked housing or bad seals which should be repaired. Refill with the recommended grade oil.
7. Grease all outside pivot points and tilt pins with a hand gun.
8. On power trim and tilt, look for leaks in the hose con-

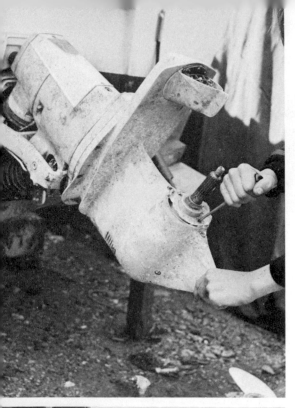

Figure 42. Replacing zinc collar on sterndrive. Outside unit should be cleaned of marine growth and painted as part of layup work.

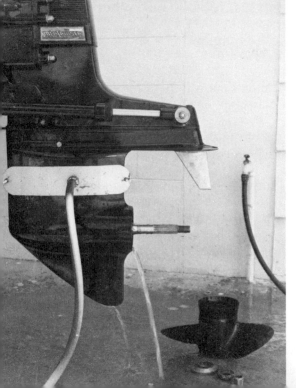

Figure 43. Flushing sterndrive housing removes rust and sediment from water passages. Adaptor plate connects hose—some units have it built-in.

nections. Clean any dirt and rust from the cylinder shafts with emery cloth.

9. Check the boot, the rubber seal at the transom, for brittleness, cracks and wear. Have a new one installed before you launch the boat. Some yards install new boots every season—regardless.

10. While the prop is off, check it for damages and if you can't fix them, bring it to a shop. If it's beyond repair, order a new one. Before you replace the prop, see if the zinc collar under it needs replacing. Use water-resistant grease on the spline when you put the wheel back on so it can be removed easily in an emergency.

11. When the outside unit of a sterndrive is removed for storage, cover and seal the transom opening before you put on a winter cover.

The Layup Above Decks

With the outside hull work completed, you can move up on deck for the layup jobs there and those aloft. These will vary for power- and sailboats, but in either case begin at the top of the rigging (powerboats have some, too) and work your way down.

MASTS, SPARS AND RIGGING

On a sailboat these are a major part of the topsides layup and, as we mentioned before, when the mast is unstepped and on the ground, it's a lot easier to do the work than going aloft. In alloy spars and masts, look for any cracks and corrosion, broken or worn fittings, enlarged fastening holes, etc. In wooden spars, check for cracks and splits, dry rot, and for similar trouble with fittings and fastenings. We covered the repairs on spars in the first section, if you want to tackle these at layup time.

On the standing rigging, examine it for broken strands, wear on the wire, corrosion if it's galvanized. When you find too many bad spots in a stretch, have a rigger replace it before the next season. Go over the spreaders and their fittings to see if any replacements are needed. Wooden ones can split beyond repair and alloy metal weaken from cracks and corrosion.

Turnbuckles are another part of the standing rigging that should be inspected for damage, especially if some eager beaver in the crew has tried to tighten them and crossed the threads. A machinist can use a die to straighten them, but replacement may be a lot cheaper. The running rigging is something you can bring home and inspect at your convenience while the boat is laid up. Make sure you tag the related parts of wire and cordage, blocks, tackle, etc. so you can rig it back in the right order. Check everything for signs of tired gear and have any replaced. You may also want to give some thought to making changes in the rigging to improve sail handling.

POWERBOAT RIGGING

This is a lot simpler than on a sailboat but it still needs some preparation for layup. For one thing, it's much easier to unstep a signal mast and lay it flat on the cabin top than try to fit a winter cover over or around it. While it's down you can also do any refinishing during storage, check wiring and lights, etc.

Removable rigging like a whip antenna, outriggers, cockpit or awning cover frames, etc. can also be taken down and stored flat under the cover. Make a mental note of any broken fittings or damage to the antenna plug so they can be fixed or repaired before the new season.

THE TOPSIDE CANVAS

This includes Bimini tops, cockpit covers, awnings, windshield and window screens, etc. You may want to use some of it to supplement a partial winter cover but it's likely to be damaged by the weather or get mildew build-up. If it's possible, take down all the canvas and store it ashore in a dry place. Check the fasteners and zippers; any rips or tears should be repaired by a canvas shop during storage. Make sure the fabric is completely dry before you fold it for storage. Canvas that's left aboard rolled up in a forepeak or stowed under berths is likely to have mould and mildew on it from the condensation under a cover. The best way is to get it all off the boat.

FLYING BRIDGE/HELM STATION LAYUP

Make a start here by taking off all the electronics and instruments that can be disconnected—radiotelephone, RDF, depth sounder, compass, etc.—and store them at home. If there were any gremlins in any of these, have a specialist check them out during the layup period. Other equipment, such as the instrument panel, engine controls, steering wheel, etc., can be covered to protect it from condensation.

With the size of some fly bridges today, there's often a raft of cushions. These can be taken off the boat for cleaning and recovering if needed. On vinyl, one of the chemical cleaners will do the job but won't bring back any fading. Spraying on a matching color and then a clear coat of lacquer will work for awhile but even this goes in time. Where the foam inside cushions has broken down, an upholsterer can replace it and make a new covering if needed.

SAILBOAT COCKPIT/HELM STATION

The layup work here is much the same as on a fly bridge —taking off removable instruments, covering those left in place, including covers for the wheel, pedestal and binnacle. The instruments taken off should be checked and serviced during storage. With tiller steering, the stick may need refinishing and can be taken off for the job. Incidentally, an outboard-hung rudder will often swing in the wind, moving the tiller unless it is lashed tight during storage.

DECKHOUSE, CABIN TOPS AND SIDES

The overall washdown may be all that's needed for layup if the fiberglass, paint or varnish in these areas is in good condition. Where the surfaces are weathered and damaged though, it's best to give them some protection during storage so the finish doesn't get any worse. Applying a light coating will safeguard it, especially if the boat is going to be left in wet storage. Where any repairs are needed on these areas, you may want to do some of them as part of the layup. This work is covered in Section 2 for all the different materials.

Where equipment is mounted on a house or cabin top, such as a searchlight, air conditioner, air horns, etc., it should be covered during storage. Ventilators and hatches should be left open to keep air moving below and to stop condensation when the winter cover is on the boat.

Details on repairing leaks in ports and windows are discussed in Section 2. This can be reviewed if you want to tackle any of these as part of the layup work. Where there is broken hardware, it should be added to your list of replacement parts so you or the yard can install them before the next season.

TRIM AND BRIGHTWORK

Here again the finish may be good enough to hold through storage but, if it looks weathered, you'll save yourself time and trouble later on by giving it a light coat of varnish now to protect it. Teak may also need attention to keep it from darkening—use one of the restorers to help keep it in good condition.

The Layup on Deck

Before you get to work on this, clean out all the loose gear from lockers, under cockpit seats and deck boxes—things like dock lines, winch handles, life preservers (also the horseshoe type from stanchions or rails), fenders, swim ladders, etc. Bring it all ashore for checking and repairs during storage.

SAILBOAT WINCHES

We went into their inspection and servicing thoroughly in Section 2. Any trouble signs like skipping or bucking may be a tipoff during the season that repairs are needed, so take the winches to a specialist while the boat is laid up. If there are no problems with them, do the cleaning and lubricating we recommended at fitting-out time. Keep covers on the winches during storage or use the plastic bucket trick to protect them.

GROUND TACKLE

Where anchors are chocked on deck or catted from a bow roller, take them below for storage. Make sure the cordage is dry and stow it separately so all the ground tackle isn't a mare's nest when you want to use it.

WINDLASSES AND CAPSTANS

These should be protected with a cover during layup (especially electric models) to keep moisture out of the wiring. For those of the old school favoring a manual model, stow the handle below in some place you'll remember next season.

LIFELINES, RAILS, STANCHIONS, LADDERS, PULPITS

Their upkeep is covered in Section 2. However, if any are too badly damaged, talk to the yard about getting them replaced. Some parts may have to be custom-welded by an outside supplier, and the off season is a good time to do it. You may also have some ideas on how improvements could be made for more safety and convenience and now is the time to work them out.

DOWN TO THE DECKS

With all the loose gear taken off for the layup, you can see if any repairs or refinishing are needed on the decks. This was given a full treatment earlier in Section 2, including suggestions for recaulking deck seams. There may still be some traditionalists in the sailing fraternity who follow the fishermen's practice of painting the decks. If you're among this breed, a light coat of paint at layup time will protect them during storage.

Where the mast has been unstepped on a sailboat, cover the opening in the deck or cabin top to protect it against leaks in the winter cover or condensation running below. Use a piece of metal over the hole but raise it slightly above the deck (like the cap on a chimney) so air can flow below and help the ventilation there.

The Layup Below

Some of the work that is usually done there for storage has been covered in Section 3 as part of the annual maintenance below decks. However, this has again been included for the jobs listed to give you the overall layup procedure. This also includes the specialized care necessary to protect the equipment against freezing in colder climates.

To simplify the layup below decks, the work has been broken down into the different areas—galley, head, cabin, etc. The engine compartment is further divided into care of gasoline and diesel engines, sterndrive prep, etc.

ENGINE COMPARTMENT

Before getting into the work here, it is important to repeat the earlier reminder to do the engine preparation while your boat is still in the water. This requires running it for short periods to change the oil, "fog" cylinders, etc., which the yard may not let you do when the boat is on land. It also requires an outside cooling-water supply to the engine to keep it from overheating. It's a lot easier to lay up an engine when the boat's afloat, so keep this in mind when you're planning the work.

The first step should be to check in your log book to see when the engines were last tuned up or overhauled. About every 250 hours for a tuneup and about 500 hours for a major overhaul on gas engines is the general rule. A diesel can go several times this on both counts; your service manual should have the recommended periods. When any engine work is needed, talk to the yard people so you can get on their work schedule.

Important: While the average owner is usually knowledge-able about servicing the engine, some of the layup work can cause serious damage if it is done incorrectly. Unless you have the expertise and experience for these jobs, play it safe and have the yard do the work.

GASOLINE ENGINES

Here are the checkpoints for getting them ready for storage:

1. *Lubrication System.* If the manufacturer recommends it, add an engine oil supplement to the crankcase and run the engine for a short time to circulate it. Drain the old oil using a hand pump in the dipstick opening if the plug at the bottom is hard to get at. Change the filter and fill with new oil, checking the level. Here again an engine oil supplement may keep deposits from forming during storage.
2. *Transmission.* Check the dipstick for fluid level and color. Any water in it will make it a cloudy tan instead of the normal purple-red, and can mean a leak in the housing which should be checked and repaired. Also test for any dirt by rubbing the fluid between your fingers. If it feels clean and the color is okay, add enough fluid to bring up the level.
3. *Rust Prevention.* Shut off the fuel supply at the tank, remove the flame arrestor from the top of the carburetor, and "fog" the engine by running it at a fast idle while you pour half a can of preventive oil in the carburetor. Let it run for a few minutes then pour in the rest of the can so it stalls the engine. To prevent rust in the cylinders, take out the plugs (be careful not to get any dirt in the holes) and carefully squirt *not more than one ounce* of crankcase detergent/rust inhibitor oil in each cylinder. Any more can be dangerous, causing hydraulic lock and damaging the engine when it is started. Replace the plugs then crank the engine with the starter for 15 seconds to coat the oil on the cylinder walls. Make

sure the high tension lead is out of the distributor and ground wire while cranking. On overhead valve engines, remove the covers and lubricate the springs and rocker arms, putting new gaskets on the covers.

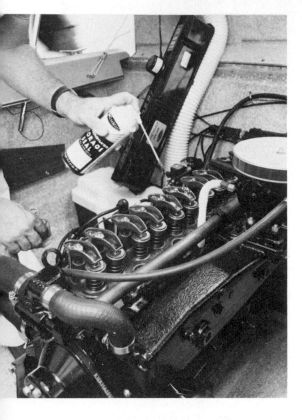

Figure 44. Coating valve rocker arms with storage seal oil stops rust and condensation. Inside of valve covers should also be given same treatment.

4. *Air Filter and Flame Arrestor.* Take both of these off the engine, put in a new filter, and clean the core of the flame arrestor by soaking it in kerosene. Dry it off and before replacing it, seal the opening with waterproof tape before putting back the filter housing.

5. *Fuel-Supply System.* Before you work on this, find out what policy the yard has (if any) on keeping fuel in the tanks. This can also affect your insurance during storage. If they require fuel to be drained, let them do it as the job is tricky and can be dangerous. It's much easier

Figure 45. Flame arrestor is sealed with waterproof tape to keep moisture and dirt out of engine. Carburetor should be cleaned and adjusted before running engine next season.

to do before the boat is hauled. Some yards will let you keep gas in the tanks and if this is the case, top them off before storage and add a conditioner to prevent formation of deposits that can gum up the carburetor. With gas in or out of the tanks, shut off the fuel line there and drain the feed to the pump and carburetor. The gas filters in the line should be cleaned, replacing any removable elements.

6. *Electrical System.* These are the parts that should be checked and prepared for the layup:

Wiring. Go over the ignition harness looking for cracks in the insulation where moisture can penetrate, putting it out of business next season. Where it's okay, give it a shot of waterproofing spray for protection. A badly cracked harness should be replaced before storage.

Distributor. Another place where condensation can get in its dirty work, especially if the cap has cracks in it. Snap it off and check; also clean the contacts inside with one of the chemical sprays for this. Take off the rotor inside looking for wear and corrosion. Trouble spots in cap or rotor mean replacing them. Also see if the breaker points are pitted or burned, and if so replace them, too. Put a few drops of oil on the rotor shaft before you replace it.

Spark Plugs. Take off the harness and remove these, checking for deposits or burned gap points. Oil on the plugs can mean worn piston rings or scored cylinder walls. A smoky exhaust will confirm this; in any event, call in a mechanic to diagnose the trouble. Some plugs may only need cleaning in a solvent if there are no problems with rings.

7. *Engine-Cooling System.* In colder climates this requires winterizing for storage which we'll get into for both sea- and fresh water cooling systems later in this section.

DIESEL ENGINES

Although some of the layup jobs on a diesel are similar to those on a gas engine, others require a different preparation for storage. Here's what is generally included to get a diesel engine ready:

1. *Lubrication.* Run the engine to get the oil warm, then drain it using a hand pump if needed. Replace the old filter and at this point it's a good idea to see if the oil pump needs cleaning. If it doesn't, refill the system with new oil following the manufacturer's service recommendation and put in an additive if suggested. Some yards do this automatically to stop gummy deposits from forming during storage. Next, run the engine to circulate the new oil then seal all lubricating oil openings, the filler and breather cap outlets with waterproof tape.

On some diesels, there's an oil cooler with built-in filters that should have the elements replaced. The heat exchanger in the cooler also has to be prepared for storage in cold climates. This will be covered under "Engine-Cooling Systems."

2. *Rustproofing.* This can be done to the engine by squirting rust-preventive oil into the blower inlet while it is running. To prevent rust and corrosion in the cylinders, remove the injectors and spray one-fourth pint of lubricating oil in each bore. Turn the engine over to form a film of this then replace the injectors.

3. *Fuel Supply.* Fill all fuel tanks with clean diesel fuel. Drain any water and sediment from the bottoms of the primary and secondary filters and replace the elements —also the gaskets on the heads. If you have the expertise, clean the transfer pump and the injection pump— if not have a pro do the job. Wrap up the work on the fuel system by sealing the fuel tank vents with waterproof tape.

4. *Air Filters and Intakes.* Take out the filters and the intake piping and blow them out to remove dirt. Where the elements are badly plugged, replace them. To dry out any moisture in the air passages put in a small bag of silica gel (like the kind used in camera cases) in the air intake. Seal all intake openings with waterproof tape.

5. *Exhaust Piping.* To keep moisture out of the manifolds, take off the exhaust pipes, clean out the rust then seal the ports with waterproof tape.

6. *Transmission.* In a diesel, this is similar to the one in a gasoline engine and should get the same care, including checking the color of the oil for any leaks in the housing. Add fluid if the level is low.

7. *Cooling System.* A fresh-water system with a heat exchanger is used on most diesels. We'll cover the winterizing of this later on.

Important: Do not start the engine with any intake openings sealed. Be sure to remove all tape coverings.

CLEANING AND PAINTING

Wrap up the engine layup by removing the grease and dirt with a chemical cleaner or having the yard steam clean the mill. Give it a coat of paint and it will be easier to spot any gasket leaks during the next season. To protect the exposed metal parts, use a rust-preventive spray on them.

Inside Sterndrive Layup

To prepare this for storage, follow the normal maintenance covered in Section 3, "The Maintenance Below."

Engine-Cooling Systems

GASOLINE AND DIESEL

These are the steps usually followed to prepare these for layup including winterizing for cold climates:

SEA-WATER SYSTEMS

1. Drain out the water completely, then flush with fresh water to remove any salt deposits, sediment and the inevitable rust. You can add chemicals to the flushing water that will help this.
2. Open the drain plugs on the block and exhaust manifolds and break any connections at low spots so you drain the system completely.
3. Replace the plugs and refill the system with 50% water, 50% antifreeze (alcohol-type not glycol which will attack rubber). Run the engine to circulate the mixture until you see color coming out the exhaust. Check the drain plugs and connections for any leaks. You can bleed any remaining water from the system at it's lowest point (it's heavier than antifreeze), then add an equal amount of the 50/50 mixture at the same point.
4. Remove the rubber impeller from the sea-water pump to avoid damage during storage.

FRESH-WATER COOLING SYSTEMS

These are similar on both gasoline and diesel engines but on some of the latter, the system not only cools the engine block through the main heat exchanger but also other exchangers (smaller ones), built into separate oil and transmission-fluid coolers. Both the main and auxiliary exchangers should be serviced and if necessary winterized, as part of the engine layup. The deterioration of any zinc plugs or rods sometimes used in them to stop galvanic corrosion should be checked and replaced.

The fresh-water systems for both gasoline and diesels normally involve the following jobs before storage:

1. Where there is already a coolant (antifreeze and water) in the fresh-water side, it doesn't need winterizing. If there isn't, drain the water, flush and drain again.
2. Repeat the operation on the sea-water side and if there's a filter in the inlet line, clean or replace the element.
3. Depending on No. 1 above, refill one or both sides of the system with 60% water, 40% antifreeze, run the engine to circulate until color comes from the exhaust.
4. Remove the rubber impeller on the sea-water pump—the fresh-water one isn't removable.
5. The heat exchangers in the system require removal and cleaning about every other year or whatever the service manual calls for.

LOOSEN THE ENGINE BELTS

These drive alternators, pumps, auxiliary generators and other equipment on marine engines. During a long storage period, the tension on them can stretch the belts and place a strain on equipment bearings, hydraulic pump rotors, etc. To prevent this, loosen all the belts but remember that you did it, otherwise when you start the engine at commissioning time, it will sound like it's tearing itself apart. The service manual for engines usually has the right amount of belt tension.

AUXILIARY GENERATOR SETS

Whatever layup treatment you give to the main engine should also be given to the one in the generator set—including the cooling system, lube oil care and filter, ignition work (for a gas engine), etc. Your log should also tell you when the auxiliary engine was last tuned up or overhauled—a lot of hours can build up with heavy cruising. If it's needed, make a date with the yard for the work. On demand systems, if the start-up has given you any headaches have it checked out and repaired.

BATTERY CARE

Regardless of the storage method for the boat, these should be taken off and kept in a warm, dry place. If left aboard, the electrolyte of a discharged battery can freeze and damage the plates in winter climates. When they're out of the engine compartment, clean off any corrosion on the cable clamps with a bicarb solution and, at the same time, check to see if they need replacing.

The best way to keep batteries in good condition during the storage period is to have them connected to a trickle charger. Use a hydrometer to check the cells and remember to leave the filler caps off so gas doesn't build up during the charging. Incidentally, some yards have a battery room with racks and a master charger to keep them up during storage.

BILGE PUMPS

Since these are usually out of sight and therefore often ignored during the season, give them a thorough inspection at layup time, including removal if possible. Check the mounting screws for corrosion—brass ones will dezincify (the metal turns into a white powder), so you may have a floating pump next season if the bad screws aren't replaced.

On submersible models, remove the housing and clean the screen below, checking the impeller for any broken blades. You can get a replacement from the dealer and it's easy to install. Some automatic models have a float switch that should be checked. If there's a strainer in the inlet to the pump, that should be cleaned.

SEACOCKS

These are other out-of-sight hardware items that may not get any maintenance during the season. While the boat is out of the water, the strainers should be cleaned. For the inside upkeep, open the seacocks to drain any water collected around them, then lubricate the valve with graphite. Be sure to close all seacocks when you finish the layup below decks —don't take a chance of forgetting it before the boat is launched next season or if you're going to store her afloat.

Winterizing the Water System

To ensure a good supply of potable water for the next season, the system needs some preparation at layup, particularly in climates where freezing temperatures can damage lines and equipment.

These are the jobs that are usually done to protect the system:

Tanks. With the variety of fresh-water conditions encountered in cruising, tanks may contain dirt and sediment that should be flushed out. When it's done, drain the tanks and supply lines completely, breaking the connections at the lowest point then tightening them back.

Hand Pumps. Those at the galley and head sinks along with the supply lines should be drained. It usually isn't necessary to fill them with antifreeze.

Pressure Systems. The best guide to laying these up is the service manual from the manufacturer. Where there's an accumulator, purifier or filter in the plumbing, the system needs a little more care. To drain the pump and these accessories, disconnect the feed lines below them. Tighten them back, making sure the shutoff valve at the tank is closed, pour in a non-toxic, antifreeze like "Winterguard" (blue color), and run the pump until the color shows at the faucets. Some owners have used vodka for this purpose which is not only expensive but can't be told from water at the tap—unless you want to indulge in flowing martinis!

Hot-Water Heaters. All types, both domestic and off-the-engine heaters, should be drained completely. If you do a good job, there's not much chance of water remaining to freeze.

Purifiers and Distilling Units. Follow the manufacturer's instructions for these—usually draining the units and lines with or without adding a non-toxic antifreeze. While you're at it, replace any removable elements in the filters.

The Galley Layup

The water supply system has already been covered, but there are other jobs to be done here before storage. Start by cleaning out anything that can smell or rust from the cabinets and under the sink—all food, cans of cleaners, soap, sponges, etc. Take all the utensils, dishes, glassware and cutlery ashore for cleaning and storage. Give all cabinets and drawers a thorough cleaning—any signs of insect life should mean spraying the interiors with an insecticide. Be sure to leave all drawers and cabinet doors open during storage.

Plumbing. Open the seacock for the sink outlet to drain it. Close the valve, then pour in regular antifreeze to fill the trap and outlet pipe. This will prevent any remaining water from freezing.

Supply Lines. These should be drained completely by disconnecting the unions at the lowest point. You can also use compressed air to blow them dry with a portable compressor or from an air line, if there's one in the yard.

Fridge and Freezer. Any leftover food should be taken out and the inside of the box cleaned with a bicarb or ammonia solution. With a mechanical compression fridge, the compressor may be sea-water cooled involving a pump and through-hull fittings. Drain this plumbing by opening the seacock—remember to close it after the layup. Air-cooled compressors don't need any preparation.

Stoves. The work here depends on the type of fuel. For gas, shut the valve at the tank and bring it ashore—*don't leave it on the boat!* Clean out the burners on the stove with a fine wire. On alcohol stoves, release the pressure on the cap, drain the tank dry and take it ashore—also, don't leave any alcohol in containers on the boat. Clean and oil the pressure pump and valves, clean out the burners.

On all stoves, spray one of the rust-preventive chemicals on the exposed metal parts. Any grease deposits in ovens should be cleaned but do it carefully if you use a spray—with plenty of ventilation. Leave the oven door open.

The Head

The layup here is similar to that in the galley but, with the variety of toilets and marine sanitation devices in use today, the work is more involved. Make your first target cleaning out the cabinets and shelves under sink counters—anything that can mould or rust. Take all towels, shower curtains, window drapes and other materials ashore for cleaning and storing.

Sink. Assuming the hand pump is already winterized, give the drain pipe and trap under the sink the same treatment. Open the seacock to drain the line, then close the valve and fill the trap with antifreeze. Next, drain the supply lines to the sink.

Shower. The supply lines to it should be drained or blown dry. To protect the drain line, get all the water out and fill it with antifreeze. Where the shower runs into a sump with an automatic pump, winterize it the same way.

Manual Toilets. Yard people will tell you one of the troubles with these during the season is improper winter layup. Using the service manual will help prevent this.

On a regular manual (hand pump) toilet, the layup generally involves these steps:

1. Close the inlet water seacock and drain all the water. Remove the inlet hose from the pump housing and temporarily attach a short hose to the inlet.
2. Pour several quarts of antifreeze (but not the alcohol or anti-leak type) into a suitable container. Insert the end of the temporary hose in it and pump until all the fluid is used. It should then be filling the toilet and discharge line.
3. Close the outlet seacock quickly and let the antifreeze remain in the toilet during storage.
4. Disconnect the temporary hose and reconnect the inlet hose to the pump housing.

These steps will protect both the inlet and discharge sides of the pump. Just pouring antifreeze in the bowl only protects the discharge side.

Important: Don't put oil, kerosene, gasoline or alcohol in the bowl or pump of a marine toilet or you'll ruin the valves.

For electric toilets, the best method is to follow the service manual. This usually involves draining all water from the system and replacing it with a suitable antifreeze that won't damage the internal parts.

Marine Sanitation Devices. Their layup depends on the type of system used so check the manufacturer's service instructions and follow it. This usually requires draining any water from the device to prevent it from freezing and damaging the unit. Some devices macerate and treat the waste with chemicals before it is pumped overboard. The treatment units generally need cleaning, flushing with water and drying at layup. Some devices may require the chemicals used (including salt and chlorine) to be removed from the unit during storage to prevent damage when it isn't in normal operation.

In a holding tank system, the waste should be pumped out before the layup and the tank and any related plumbing drained completely. Using a chemical deodorant in the tank during storage will help keep odors from forming. The service manuals that come with most tank systems usually details the preparation steps for layup.

FIRE EXTINGUISHERS

The normal maintenance of these is covered in the previous section. At layup time when all the work on the boat has been finished, leave one extinguisher aboard, just in case, but take the rest of the portables to be inspected and recharged. Get one ready as soon as possible to replace the one left aboard.

Any fixed extinguishing systems built into engine or fuel tank compartments are best serviced by a specialist in this work. You may be able to do a few of the jobs at layup but any maintenance of the valves and controls needs a pro.

Cabin and Deckhouse Layup

These are the places that get a lot of living in during the season and the interior furnishings may show it in wear and a tacky look. They're also the areas where a little more time spent on them before storage will mean a lot less work at fitting-out.

THE TAKE-ASHORES

By getting as many of the removable furnishings off the boat before storage, there'll be more working room for painting and repairs before she goes back in the water. Try to get off things like deck chairs, tables, cushions, books (which can get mouldy), televisions and radios that can be affected by condensation under a winter cover.

Drapes, curtains and loose covers can also be taken off for cleaning or replacement, if too far gone. Use a chemical spray to freshen up vinyl material and a foam-type on fabrics. Rugs and carpets may also be among the removables— for cleaning and storage in a dry place ashore. It's a good idea to have all floor coverings of this type removable so any damp areas under them can be left to dry and thus prevent dry rot. Shag rugs which are popular with many boat builders are a catchall for sand and dirt, difficult to dry and a general nuisance aboard.

LOCKERS, CABINETS AND DRAWERS

Remember to take off all foul-weather gear, clothing and the general trivia that builds up in these places. Leave the doors, lids and drawers open to ventilate the space below decks. Matches and flammable cleaning fluids are other nixies during storage. Charts and navigation instruments are obviously removables and don't forget portable lights—if you don't take them ashore, remove the batteries. Incidentally, the bases of light bulbs may corrode in the sockets so take these out and store them some place on board.

BERTHS AND BEDDING

Strip off everything you can, blankets, sheets, even mattresses to be cleaned or laundered and stored ashore. If the foam in the mattresses is starting to crumble, have it replaced and if you had any complaints about the thickness, get it beefed up at the same time.

VENTILATION

We went into this in an earlier section but its importance in laying up a boat for storage can't be stressed enough. Under a cover, the extremes of temperature in northern climates, from the hot sun by day to freezing cold at night, can produce an incredible amount of condensation in the hull— enough to damage just about everything there, including wood, metal and fabrics. It can even cause dry rot.

The best defense against attack by moisture is to have as much ventilation as possible—open up everything below decks. In this way, there'll be a natural flow of air from the vents in the cover down into the hull. To make sure it gets down into the bilges, take up the panels in the cabin sole or deckhouse floor and leave them off during storage. Overall carpeting can stop this air flow so have the yard cut in access panels or do it yourself if you're handy with tools.

While you can't stop all the condensation from forming below, it can be controlled in several ways. Where electric current is available in the yard, a room dehumidifier may be installed and the moisture it collects can be drained through the hole for a bottom plug or out a seacock. On smaller boats, burning a light or two below will help keep the cabin dry. There are also chemical dryers like "Air-Dri" which absorb moisture with a renewable cannister of calcium chloride or other absorbent material.

Mildew is another enemy when a boat is laid up. It can be removed from surfaces with a chemical spray but the simplest way is to keep it from forming. After you've cleaned places like counter tops and the insides of drawers and lockers, brush on a solution of formaldehyde to stop mildew spores from forming and also act as a disinfectant.

FOREPEAK AND SAIL LOCKER

This is another space below decks, usually crammed into the bow, that needs some preparation before storage. The first thing is to take ashore anything condensation can damage. Sails should be put in bags and kept in a warm dry space, ground tackle blocked up to let air circulate beneath it, cordage too. Any loose gear that doesn't belong there, old canvas and lines, etc. should come off the boat.

Ventilation is important in a forepeak so keep a hatch or ventilators in the deck open. If you need more air below, add another ventilator as described in Section 3.

Covers and Frames

When you talk to boatyard operators about layup and stor-age, many will tell you much of the damage and deteriora-tion in a boat happens *after* it is hauled and stored under a cover. The reason is that the cover acts as an incubator that breeds condensation in the hull. And this is true in most kinds of outdoor storage—on land or afloat.

The basic function of a cover is to provide protection from the weather—ice and snow in the North, the sun in warmer climates. In addition, it must be fireproof and also treated to prevent mildew and rot, well supported and have built-in ventilation.

The dealer or builder can usually furnish a custom-made cover and frame for the boat as an option. On smaller boats, stock covers fit reasonably well. When replacements are needed, a sailmaker or canvas shop can tailor one to fit—let them do the measuring so the fit is their worry, not yours. Some of the yards often rent covers for the storage period and make an additional charge for the supporting framework which can be reused each year.

WHAT MAKES A GOOD COVER?

As a general rule, to offer the most protection a cover should be at least two feet longer than the overall length of the boat and a minimum of four feet wider than the greatest beam. Even more than this if you want to bring it well down over the topsides. It's better to have the cover slightly bigger than needed, provided it doesn't sag and create hollows where water can collect. Stretching a skimpy cover to fit isn't a good idea, either.

The fabric should permit free air circulation through it and have a frame that supports it over deck structures. Some means of ventilation must be built into the cover to stop condensation in the hull. Make sure it has enough pitch to shed water (and snow, too) and that the lashings keep it tight and snug. A means of access inside the cover is important to check on the boat during storage.

Figure 46. Winter cover is carried down over sides to protect hull. Canvas should be well-secured with lashings.

Figure 47. Stern vents provide ventilation under cover to prevent condensation inside boat. This cover has a good runoff pitch and access to hull by grommets and lacing.

THE FABRICS USED

The cover material is important not only for weather protection but also to help stop condensation beneath it. Woven fabrics are popular, and among natural fibers, cotton is the granddaddy of them all because it "breathes" and lets air flow through. A good grade of canvas is 13-ounce Army duck which comes treated to resist mildew and rot but which should also be waterproofed. The best color is white which reflects the sun and prevents the heat that is generated under darker colors.

Synthetic fibers are not used as much because of their higher cost and poorer porosity. Most of these have a silicone finish to increase the water repellency but this reduces air circulation and needs more ventilation built into the cover. Dacron is sometimes used on smaller boats and occasionally on bigger ones when "seconds" of the material (slight stains making it unsuitable for sails) are available at lower cost.

Coated fabrics, usually vinyl over canvas, are not suitable for covers without a lot of vents as there is no air circulation through the material. The table of Marine Fabrics listed in Section 2, gives the advantages and disadvantages along with their typical uses and may be helpful in selecting a cover material.

Plastic is also used for covers—usually clear, polyethylene about 6 mils (.006 in.) thick and in heavier thicknesses. While it is lower in cost than other materials, there are some disadvantages. For one thing, it must be fastened to the supporting frame without nails or staples, usually by battens—that means more work putting up the covers. The film is easily cut or pierced and any break makes it vulnerable to further tearing by the wind. The biggest drawback is it requires much more ventilation, usually leaving it completely open at the bottom so snow or rain will get under the cover. Plastic is also used for free-standing covers (like a greenhouse) over the entire boat permitting the owner or yard people to work under them in wet weather.

THE FRAME

This supports the cover to clear any deck structures and should have an overhang at bow and stern for ventilation. A good frame has a husky ridgepole or strongback, with well-braced cross members and enough pitch to shed water. It's a good idea to number mating parts of the frame to help with the erection and dismantling. Use bolts for the assembly and pad any sharp edges to avoid chafing of the cover. Old carpet works well for this. A coat of paint will make the frame last longer and put your boat's name on so it will be available at the end of the season.

VENTILATION—AGAIN

This has been mentioned several times before but it is an abolute necessity under a cover. While the overhang will produce some circulation of air, there should also be a positive exchange from built-in vents. The best places for these are at the high points, bow and stern. Several types are used, including one that works on the airfoil principle to admit air without water. The flow from vents can be helped by keeping all hatches and doors open during storage.

Whatever vents are used in the cover, the idea is to equalize the outside and inside temperatures so that on a winter's day there won't be zero degrees outside and 50 degrees within from the sun's heat. When this happens the warm air under the cover condenses on the cold surfaces of the boat, forming gallons of water in a short time. In Sun Belt climates, the vents in the cover will exhaust some of the heat under it so the boat doesn't cook like an oven, warping the planking and opening up seams in a wooden hull.

ACCESS PANELS AND LASHINGS

These are two points often overlooked in storing a boat under a cover. A removable panel or two, make it convenient to get inside the hull without taking off half the canvas. Good locations are near a companionway, a door to the deckhouse or at the cockpit. The panels are usually secured with a light line laced through grommets as in a shoe—the same as most closures at bow and stern.

To keep the cover in place and the fabric tight so rain pockets don't form, lashings should run under the hull from one side to the other or at least down to the cradle. When this can't be done, use weights like short lengths of timber, bleach bottles filled with sand or concrete blocks to anchor the cover.

HOW TO MAKE A COVER LAST LONGER

Here are a few suggestions to keep in mind:

- Use as much care taking it off as you did putting it on.
- Wash off all dirt and let the fabric dry thoroughly before it is folded and stored in a dry place.
- Repair any rips or tears before you put it away. Use patch kits for small ones—have a canvas man do biggies.
- Letter your boat's name on the outside folds if you store the cover in a yard during the season.

Keeping a boat bundled up with a good cover during storage can add years of service to her life.

REMEMBER TO CHECK THE BOAT

With all the time and effort spent on the layup, it only makes good sense to see it is going well by making a regular inspection during storage. Take enough time to go aboard and see that everything is in good order.

Check the outside first to make sure the cover lashings are tight and with no puddles of water to freeze in a cold snap. Get under the cover and look for any signs of leaks—telltale water on decks that can form ice and damage fiberglass or wood. Go below and make a sniffing tour. A stale musty smell may be the clue to condensation—soggy fabrics and wet surfaces on counters will mean you need more ventilation under the cover, so try to work it out. If you've used the "Dri-Air" units we mentioned earlier to absorb moisture, see if the chemicals are still soft—if they're hard they need replacing.

Check the engine compartment for any gas fumes from any residual leaking from the fuel system. And give the bilges a quick scan for water from a topside leak or oil from the engine. All this may sound like you're hunting for trouble which is exactly what you should do at least several times during storage. You may be able to spot something still in the bud and prevent it from coming to full bloom.

Winning the Game

In the beginning of this book, we compared maintenance to a game—"keeping up the boat"—which every owner soon learns to play. And now as we come to the end of the guide, we hope it has helped you to win.

Like many games, it can have rich rewards not only in dollars saved but in a job well done that will mean a safer, more enjoyable life for you to enjoy on your boat.

There is always a new season to look forward to and new waters to explore. May you have fair winds and calm seas to sail in all those that lie ahead.